From Vladimir to Vladimir

A History of Russia-Ukraine Relations

Minneapolis
SECOND EDITION December 2022

From Vladimir to Vladimir: A History of Russia-Ukraine Relations
Copyright © 2022 by Stephen J. Vicchio.
All rights reserved.

10 9 8 7 6 5 4 3 2

Cover and interior design: Gary Lindberg
ISBN: 978-1-959770-40-4

*This book is dedicated to my friend Irene Burell,
extraordinary shopper, cleaner and devoted friend.*

Contents

Introduction 1

Part One: The Origins of Kievan Rus' 5
    Introduction. 5
    The Role of Vladimir I and the Slavic Gods 6
    Conversion of Vladimir and the Slavs to Christianity 8
    Influences of Vladimir After His Death. 11
    Conclusions to Part One 13

Part Two: The Interim Period. 17
    Introduction. 17
    The Mongol Invasion: Thirteenth Century. 17
    Polish and Lithuanian Invasion: Sixteenth Century 20
    Early Years of the Russian Czars 24
    Conclusions to Part Two 30

Part Three: The Russian Revolution to the end
    of World War II 33
    Introduction 33
    Causes and Events of the Russian Revolution 34
    Main Events of the Russian Revolution 44
    Stalin's Role in World War II 45
    Conclusions to Part Three. 50

Part Four: The Cold War: 1945 to 1991 53
    Introduction. 53
    History of the Cold War: 1945 to 1991 56
    Dissolution of the Soviet Union: 1988 to 1991 60
    Main Reasons for the Collapse of the Soviet Union. 61
    Final Days of the Soviet Union. 63
    Conclusions to Part Four. 65

Part Five: Vladimir Putin and His War in Ukraine 69
    Introduction. 69
    The Life and Times of Vladimir Putin. 70
    Putin and the War in Ukraine: 2022 72

Why Does Vladimir Putin Want Ukraine?. 74
Is There a Way Out of the War in Ukraine? 76
Does Putin Have Designs Beyond Ukraine? 78
Conclusions to Part Five 79

Part Six: The Role of Religion in the Russia-Ukraine War 83
Introduction. 83
Religion in the Soviet Empire: Some History. 84
Three Main Faiths in the Soviet Union and Ukraine: 1953 to 1991 . . 86
Putin on Religion and its Role in the War in Ukraine 87

Part Seven: Some Conclusions of this Study 93
Introduction. 93
Conclusions to Part One 93
Conclusions to Part Two 94
Conclusions to Part Three. 95
Conclusions to Part Four. 97
Conclusions to Part Five 98
Conclusions to Part Six. 101

Postscript 105

Appendix I: When Will the War in Ukraine End?. 115
Introduction. 115
Outcomes and Results So Far of the War in Ukraine. 116
Four Scenarios for the End of War in Ukraine. 118
De Facto Partition 118
Neutrality with Sweeteners. 120
The New Russian Empire Solution. 121
Final Thoughts 124

Appendix II: Foreign Words and Phrases 126

Appendix III: Summary of Events from the Collapse of the
    Soviet Union until the War in Ukraine. 129

Major Sources of this Essay. 131

Endnotes. 134

Index 153

About the Author 159

Also by Stephen J. Vicchio

Muslim Slaves in the Chesapeake: 1634 to 1865
Mala'ika: Angels in Islam
Evil and Suffering in the Bible
The Akedah or Sacrifice of Isaac
Evil in World Religions
Alexander Hamilton's Religion
The Idea of the Demonic

From Vladimir to Vladimir

A History of Russia-Ukraine Relations

Stephen J. Vicchio, Ph.D.

Wisdom
Editions

Minneapolis, Minnesota

Vladimir the Great

Introduction

This is a book about the long and complicated relationship between Russia and Ukraine. We will unfold our comments about this relationship in the six parts described in the outline above. Central to each of these parts is a Russian or Ukrainian historical figure who was important for understanding the historical relation, as well as the relationship since 1991 when the Soviet Union collapsed, and Ukraine declared its independence.

The first of our historical periods at the beginning of what was known as the Kievan Rus' was established by Vladimir I (950–1015), the Grand Prince of the kingdom, around the year 1000 AD. Thus, Part One will be devoted to the origins of Russia and Ukraine and the person of Vladimir the Great.[1]

The second period of our analysis of Russia-Ukraine relations we shall call the "Interim Period." This period lasted from the thirteenth to the nineteenth century. It was a time when Russia and Ukraine went through a series of invasions, beginning with the Mongols in the thirteenth century, followed by the invasion of the area by the Poles and Lithuanians in the sixteenth century.[2] These two invasions were followed by the annexation of Ukraine by Russia in 1793 and the movement in Ukraine called "Russification" for the entire nineteenth century.[3]

When the Polish-Lithuanian armies invaded from the west, it prompted a war between the Polish-Lithuanian Commonwealth and the czardom of Russia, and lands of the east of the Dnieper River were under Russian control. The east became known as the "Left Bank" of Ukraine, while lands to the west of the Dnieper were ruled by Poland and were called the "Right Bank" of Ukraine.

More than a century later, in 1793, the Right Bank, or Western Ukraine, was annexed by the Russian Empire during the reign of Catherine the Great of Russia. What followed in the next century and a half was the Russification of Ukraine, where the use of the Ukrainian language was banned, and the Ukrainian people were pressured to convert to the Russian Orthodox faith.

Mongol leader Genghis Khan (1162–1227) and his son Jochi Khan (1182–1227) were the most prominent figures of this Interim Period. The Mongols were very skillful horsemen. Conquering large swaths of land was much easier in the saddle. Later, a third member of the family, Batu Khan (1205–1255), also captured much territory for the Mongolian Empire.

Eventually, the empire included territory from Mongolia to Eastern Europe, an area that came to be known as the "Steppe." The term steppe originally referred to the tall, grassy plain of flat land in a temperate zone. Later, it became synonymous with the "Eurasian Steppe."[4]

In the third part of this work, we will discuss the period from the Russian Revolution in 1917 until World War II. This period saw the forming of the Soviet Union. It also included the genocide conducted by Josef Stalin in the 1930s, known as "holodomor."[5] The two prominent figures of importance during this time were Josef Stalin and Ukrainian hero Stepan Bandera.[6]

One of the most interesting questions about this time was the differing views about the relationship of Ukraine with the Nazis. Some Russians, like Vladimir Putin and his followers, thought the Ukrainians were collaborators with Hitler and his Nazi regime, while others disagreed.

As the Russian assault on Ukraine entered its second month in March of 2022, Russian President Vladimir Putin made claims that his military action was, among other things, aimed at the de-Nazification of Ukraine. At the same time, Russian foreign minister Sergei Lavrov went far enough to call Ukrainian President Zelensky a Nazi and a Neo-Nazi.

Scholar Grzegorz Rossolinski-Liebe wrote an essay entitled "Putin's Abuse of History: Ukrainian 'Nazis,' 'Genocide,' and Fake

Threat Scenario." In the essay, Rossolinski-Liebe explored the place of Nazism and historical genocide in early twentieth-century Ukraine. The writer's major conclusion is that Mr. Putin holds an abusive view of history, as well as the idea of genocide in Ukraine in the twentieth and twenty-first centuries. As Rossolinski-Liebe has it, Putin wishes to de-Nazify a country that has next to no Nazis among its current population.[7]

The fourth part of this work will contain our observations starting from the end of World War II in 1945 until the dissolution of the Soviet Union in 1991. We shall call this the Cold War period. The central figures in the fourth chapter will be a series of premieres of the Soviet Union, including Josef Stalin; Georgy Malenkov, who lost power to Nikita Khrushchev after only a few weeks; Yuri Andropov; Konstantin Chernenko, who died barely a year after taking office and was succeeded by Mikhail Gorbachev, who was president when the Soviet Union collapsed in late December 1991. Each of these five men, for various reasons, played a decisive role in the ending of the Soviet Empire.[8]

Finally, in part five of this work, we shall describe and discuss the contemporary period of Russia-Ukraine relations from 1991 to the present. There are many players, but certainly, the two most important today are Vladimir Putin and Volodymyr Zelensky. Among the questions to be raised in the fifth chapter of this work is whether Russia's invasion of Ukraine is responsible for rising gasoline prices and inflation in the United States, as the Biden Administration claims.

These five parts will be followed by a summary of the conclusions of the work, as well as raising several important questions about the contemporary relationship between Russia to Ukraine.

This brings us to Part One, where we will discuss the origins of Kievan Rus' and Vladimir I, who was the progenitor of what was to become the Russian Empire beginning around 1000 CE.

Yaroslav the Wise, son of Vladimir the Great

Part One
The Origins of the Kievan Rus'

The Kievan Rus' was the early, mostly East Slavic state dominated by the city of Kiev from about 800 CE until the middle
of the twelfth century.

—New World Encyclopedia

Summon the executioner. What is a Russian wedding without
having many fights?

—Prince Vladimir I of Kiev

Introduction

To begin the story of the relationship between Russia to Ukraine, we
must return to the period from about 800 CE when people speaking
Slavic dialects began to be called the *Rus'*, also referred to as the
"Ancient Russians," and the "Ruthenians." Later these people diverged
into three major groups or nations that today are called Belarus, Russia
and Ukraine.[9]

Additionally, there were several minor ethnic groups, including the
Carpatho-Ruthenians and several other smaller Slavic ethnic peoples.
We begin, however, by stating from the start that the Kievan Rus' is
considered the predecessor of three modern Slavic nations—Belarus,
Russia and Ukraine.

The first part of this opening section is to introduce and discuss
the reigns of Vladimir I, or Vladimir the Great (980–1015), and his
son Yaroslav I, or Yaroslav the Wise (1019–1055). These two figures

are considered the Golden Age of the Slavic peoples. It also saw the acceptance of Orthodox Christianity, as well as the creation of the first East Slavic written legal code known as the *Russkaya Pravda*.[10]

The Role of Vladimir I and the Slavic Gods

Vladimir I, the Grand Prince of Kiev, was the most prominent political and military figure in late medieval Russia. During his rule, Christianity was adopted in the Slavic states. Vladimir is also known as Saint Vladimir, Vladimir the Baptist, and Vladimir, the Red Sun.[11]

He was born around 956 CE. Vladimir's father was Svyatoslav, the Grand Prince of Kiev, who died in 972.[12] Vladimir was the youngest of his three sons. According to legend, Vladimir's mother, a woman named Malusha, was a maid for Vladimir's grandmother, Olga, with whom Vladimir spent his childhood. By the time of his birth, she was one of the first of Kievan Rus' to be baptized into Orthodox Christianity. This became very important later when Vladimir had to choose a new religion different from traditional ancient, Slavic polytheism.[13]

Slavic polytheism was not much different from the versions in ancient Greece and Rome, with many gods, each with a particular domain—the sky, war, fertility, the wind, the sun and many others. For Kievan Rus', seven principal gods were worshiped. The god *Perun* was the god of the sky, thunder and war. He was Vladimir's favorite and was considered the most powerful of the gods and had a high place in the temple of the gods.

The god named *Dazhbog*, whose name means "Giver," was in charge of dishing out wealth and providing rays of the sun. He is often depicted with a sun halo around his head and a sun orb in his hand. Every day, he is born again with the rise of the sun and dies with the sunset, only to be reborn the next morning with the sunrise.

A third ancient god of the Kievan Rus' is the son of Perun. His name was *Dzbog* and is the god of winds. He looks like an old man and is often shown holding a hunting horn used to call the winds.

The Slavic god named *Semargl* was the deity of fire and fertility. He had the ability to change shapes rapidly. He is sometimes depicted as a young Slav warrior or a winged dog or lion. He also had the ability to fly and was believed to be very intelligent and fast in his movements.

The only female god in the Slavic pantheon was *Mokosh*. She was the goddess of fate and protector of women in childbirth. Mokosh enjoyed wandering Earth dressed as an old woman and pestered people in their homes during Lent.[14]

The god *Veles* for the Slavs was the ruler of the Underworld and the harvests and was the deity that brought cattle and other animals to people. Veles was usually shown as a wooly, hairy, dark figure associated with magic, music and treachery. Veles was also the enemy of Perun. He can be found in virtually every Slavic pantheon, from Kievan Rus' to the Balkans, as well as in central Europe. While he is generally considered to be sinister, in fact, in later Slavic literature, he took on the role of a demonic figure and was considered to be associated with the devil in the Russian Orthodox Church.[15]

There is no doubt that Veles was in high regard by the Slavs. He was a prominent figure in their mythology, especially among Eastern and Southern Slavs. Veles is the only god, except for Perun, who was respected and adored among all Slavic tribes.

The most often told story or myth about Veles has the demon transformed into a snake and then slithers up Perun's oak tree, the opposite of Veles' willow tree. As he climbed the tree, Veles entered Perun's home in the sky. In some versions, Veles kidnaps Yarilo, Perun's tenth son. Then Veles brings him back to the Underworld, but he does not torture nor kill him. Instead, he raises Yarilo as his own son. Eventually, Yarilo also becomes a figure of the Underworld.

Needless to say, Perun was not happy about his son's kidnapping, and this is what led to what the Slavs call the "Myth of the Great Storm." It tells the tale of a great battle between Perun and Veles. The two titans clashed in a huge thunderstorm which is why Veles, at times, is also associated with storms.[16]

The battle began when Veles crawled out of the Underworld and again tried to slither up Perun's oak tree. Perun responded by casting thunderbolts at the giant snake. The demon then responded by shape-shifting into various other animals, people and kinds of trees. At the end of the Great Storm, Perun prevails and manages to kill the Great Serpent of the Great Storm.[17]

Finally, a seventh god of the ancient Slavs was named *Rod*. Rod was the creator of all things that exist, including the other gods. It is said that he came to Earth in a golden egg and hatched himself like a baby chick. After he had created everything on Earth, he looked around and realized something was missing. So he breathed on the ground, and his consort *Lada*, the goddess of love, was born.[18]

Lada also appeared as a hatched egg, and when the egg was broken, love spilled out. Then legend tells us that Rod finished his work and promptly disappeared. This may be why he did not have a place in Vladimir's temple that housed the Slavic pantheon.

This brings us to the conversion of Vladimir to Orthodox Christianity, the topic of the next section of Part One, followed by another section, followed by more on the place of Vladimir on the origins of the Slavic peoples, including Russians and Ukrainians.

Conversion of Vladimir and the Slavs to Christianity

Vladimir I became the ruler of Kievan Rus' after overthrowing his brother Yaropolk in 978. At that time, Vladimir formed an alliance with Basil II of the Byzantine Empire. In fact, he married Basil's sister, Anna, in 988.

Church of the Tithes

After this marriage, Vladimir officially changed the state religion from polytheism, discussed in the previous section, to Orthodox Christianity. In the process, he destroyed all the temples and icons devoted to those gods. A year later, Vladimir built the first stone church in Kiev in 989, which he called "the Church of the Tithes."[19]

According to available documents from this time, Vladimir sent envoys to investigate the religions of the people around Kievan Rus'. The envoys who returned from Constantinople reported that the festivities and the presence of God in the Christian Orthodox faith were more beautiful than any other religion.[20]

In addition to sending ambassadors to Constantinople, Vladimir sent envoys to the Jewish Khazars and the Muslim Bulgars. He chose Orthodox Christianity because his ambassadors reported to him after visiting that the Cathedral of Holy Wisdom, or the *Hagia Sophia*, in Constantinople was a "wonder to perceive." The ambassadors reported to Vladimir:

> We knew not whether we were in Heaven or simply on the Earth. For on Earth, there is no such splendor or such beauty...We cannot forget that beauty.[21]

Another point of view or interpretation of these facts suggested that Basil II needed a military and political ally in the face of skirmishes in Constantinople. In this version of the story, Vladimir demanded the royal marriage in exchange for military assistance. He also promised Basil that he would convert. Basil's response was in order to marry Anna, Vladimir would have to be baptized in the Orthodox faith. This second perspective is generally taken by Islamic scholars.

When Vladimir returned to Kiev in 988, he gathered all the people on the banks of the Dnieper River, at which time they were solemnly baptized. This year is marked the beginning of the Slavic Orthodox Church and the time that Kievan Rus' became a metropolis of the Patriarch of Constantinople. In Kiev, the mass baptism went smoothly, but it was a different story in Novgorod, the second largest Slavic city.

In Novgorod, the people rebelled against the idea of baptism and refused to give up their polytheism, temples and icons. Vladimir's troops suppressed an uprising in Novgorod, but the ancient polytheism continued to be practiced in parts of Russia for several more centuries.

The city of Novgorod at the time was ruled by Vladimir's brother, Prince Yaroslav. In the course of the Battle of Berestovov, however, Vladimir died near Kiev on July 15, 1015.[22]

Vladimir I completed the unification of all eastern Slavs in his realm. He secured his frontiers against foreign invasions, and by accepting Christianity, he brought the Slavic nations into the community of Christian nations and Christian civilization.

Vladimir was remembered and celebrated in many legends and songs as a great national hero and ruler. He was called the Baptizer of Russia, a man who "was equal to the apostles." Vladimir was canonized in the middle of the thirteenth century by the Orthodox Church. After Vladimir's death, a church was erected in his honor called the Church of the Savior in Berestovo. It is north of the Monastery of the Caves. It is also the church where Yuri Dolgoruky, the founder of Moscow, was interred.[23]

Vladimir I has been canonized in the Orthodox Church, even though the requirement of three miracles for sainthood was relaxed, and in its stead, transformations in the life of Vladimir were offered as evidence. Although other Orthodox saints are credited with healings from illness, deliverance from passion, and rebirth of the sinful, the Slavs believe that all of Vladimir's miracles were performed on himself. If there were any miracles reported at his gravesite, which is customary, he might well have been called a god rather than a saint.[24]

Both Vladimir and his grandmother Olga are honored as the founders of Russian Orthodox Christianity. Various parts of Vladimir's dismembered body were distributed among many churches and monasteries he had established and were venerated as icons and relics.

Indeed, many of these early churches remain key institutions in Russian Orthodoxy. Saint Volodymyr's Cathedral in Kiev is dedicated to him, as was the University of Kiev. There is also the Order of Saint Vladimir in Russia and the Saint Vladimir's Orthodox Theological Seminary in the United States in Yonkers, New York.[25]

The original Kiev Rus' was an empire comprised of hundreds of small towns and ethnic regions, each with its own Nordic-Slavic polytheism and religious practices. Vladimir's main goal was to integrate these towns and cities into one Slavic empire.

Even before Vladimir, however, the Byzantine patriarch Photius sent a letter in the year 867 that described what was called the Rus'-Byzantine War of 860 AD. According to Photius, the people of the region appeared to be enthusiastic about their new religion. Photius also sent a bishop to convert the Slavs, but it was another twenty years before Vladimir I completed that goal.[26]

This brings us to the third section of this first chapter, in which we will describe the influence of Vladimir I after his death on July 15, 1015. This is the final section of Chapter One.

Influences of Vladimir After His Death

By the time of Vladimir's death, his empire stretched from beyond Novgorod in the north to beyond the city of Kiev in the south. At the empire's greatest extent in the mid-eleventh century—thirty-five years after Vladimir's death—the Kievan Rus' empire stretched from the White Sea in the north to the Black Sea in the south and from the headwaters of the Vistula in the west to the Taman peninsula in the east. This was the greatest extent of the early unification of the Slavic peoples.

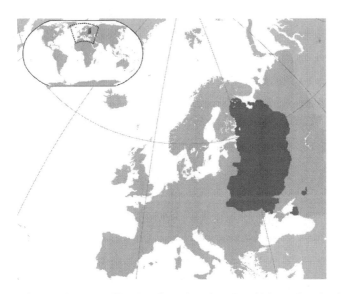

A map of later Kievan Rus', after the death of Yaroslav in 1054.

After the death of Vladimir, a bloody war ensued among his sons regarding who was in charge of the kingdom. His one son, Yaroslav the Wise, was ultimately the victor over another son, Sviatopolk, who had killed two other sons of Vladimir named Boris and Gleb. These latter two sons became known as canonized saints in the Russian Orthodox Church. Boris and Gleb were given the nickname "passion bearers."[27] Earlier, both Vladimir and his grandmother Olga also were canonized.[28] Vladimir's moniker became "equal to the Apostles" because of his role in Christian conversion.[29]

Vladimir Putin has referred to Prince Vladimir as the "Savior of Russia." And he has promoted the religious cult of the prince. For Putin, both Kiev and Crimea—where Putin was baptized—are considered "sacred lands." This may tell us a great deal about why Vladimir annexed Crimea in 2014. It is his "hometown," if you will. A large statue of Vladimir I now stands next to the Kremlin. During the unveiling of the statue on November 4, 2016, Mr. Putin told the large crowd assembled there:

> Vladimir the Great laid the moral foundations on which our lives are still based today. It was a strong moral bearing solidarity and unity that held our ancestors...wing victories for the fatherland, making it stronger and greater with each generation.

Today, Vladimir Putin sees the beginning of Russia, Ukraine, Moldova, as well as many other Slavic ethnic peoples, as having begun as one people. He also believes, as we shall see later in this study, that the original Kievan Rus' dynasty had at least eleven different principalities that included: Kiev, Novgorod, Cheringov, Pereyaslavl, Suzdal, Volhyniya, Halych, Polotsk, Smolensk, as well as Ryazan, and Mongol. During its existence, Kievan Rus' was known as *Ar-Rus'* among the Arabs. In Old French, it was called *Russie* and Latin as *Rusia* or *Russia*, from which we get the English word "Russia." The Germans spelled the name of the Slavic empire as as *Ruscia* or *Ruzzia*.[30]

Various other etymologies have been proposed, including the Finnish *Ruotsi*, as well as the Swedish *Ros*, the name of a tribe from the middle Dnieper Valley region. In fact, many linguists attributed the name Kievan Rus' derives from an Old Norse term *Rods*, meaning "men who row," because rowing was the central method of navigating the rivers of Eastern Europe.[31]

This brings us to the conclusions of this first part. The second part of our analysis we shall call the "Interim Period," but traditional Russian historians often refer to the period as the "Dark Ages."

Conclusions to Part One

We have divided the first part of this work into an introduction, in which we have sketched out the content of this work as having five major parts. This was followed by Part One of this analysis of the relation of Russia to Ukraine. We divided Part One into three sections—an introduction to Prince Vladimir of Kiev, the progenitor of Russia and Ukraine.

In the second section of Part One, we discussed the conversion of Vladimir and his kingdom from Nordic-Slavic polytheism to a kingdom devoted to the Eastern Orthodox Church, centralized in Constantinople and the figure of Basil II.[32]

In the third section of Part One, we made some observations about the influence that Vladimir had on the Slavic peoples. In that section, we made two principal observations. First, we discussed the geographical extent of the Kievan Rus' empire, that was at its furthest extent around the mid-eleventh century.[33] Photius (810–891) was the ecumenical patriarch of Constantinople from 858 until 867. He is known as Saint Photius the Great in the Eastern Orthodox Church. One of his claims to fame was his voluminous knowledge of Greek literature and philosophy. He is sometimes called "The leading intellectual of his time, the leading light of the ninth-century renaissance."[34]

Secondly, we discussed the internal wars among the sons of Vladimir and the ultimate control of the kingdom by one son named Yarolslav, also called "The Wise" by the Orthodox Church.

Additionally, we mentioned some comments made recently by Vladimir Putin about Prince Vladimir I and his kingdom, particularly about the moral foundations of the early Slavic empire in the eleventh century.

Finally, in Part One, we made some remarks about the etymology of the names of the early Slavic kingdom, as well as what it was called by the Arabs, Greeks, Romans, and the Nordic people. In fact, we supplied the names of what Vladimir's kingdom and people have been called by the Arabs, French, English, Swedish, Germans and by other Eurasian peoples.[35]

This brings us to Part Two, what we have called the "Interim Period," or the "Dark Ages," by the Slavs. In this section, we will discuss a series of invasions or annexations by other Eurasian people, beginning with the Mongols, then the Poles and Lithuanians in the sixteenth century, and the annexation of Ukraine by the Russians in 1793.[36]

Genghis Khan

Part Two
The Interim Period

If you had not committed great sins, God would not have sent
a punishment like me upon you.

—Genghis Khan

Why is it that the Mongols of the world always tell us they are
defending the rest of us against the Mongols?

—Nostradamus

Introduction

We have labeled this second part about the history of the relationship between Russia and Ukraine the "Interim Period." We have given it that name because, between the twelfth and late eighteenth centuries, Slavic history was mainly about various ethnic groups who attempted to conquer Kievan Rus', including Ukraine. These invasions involved the Mongols in the twelfth and thirteenth centuries and the Polish and Lithuanians in the sixteenth century. Thus, Part Two will have three main sections—the Mongols, the Polish and Lithuanians, and the Russian annexation of Ukraine in the eighteenth century.[37]

The Mongol Invasion: Thirteenth Century

From 1237 to 1241, an eastern nomadic people known as the Mongols conquered most of modern Russia with the aid of their Turkish allies. Although the Mongols in their heyday were pluralistic, the Turks aided them because they tended to be monotheistic. Later in their history, the

Mongols did convert to Islam, which added strength to their bond with Turkey.

At the time of the Mongol invasion, Kievan Rus' was divided politically and socially by its numerous principalities. They could offer only moderate resistance to the Mongols, as the invaders killed thousands, conquering one Russian town and city after another.[38]

In many ways, the Mongol invasion could be compared to the fifth-century CE incursion of Germanic tribes into the Western Roman Empire. Before advancing into Russia, however, the Mongols had already conquered and slaughtered a large swathe of Asia by the early thirteenth century.[39]

After the Mongols took control of Russia, they continued west into Poland, Hungary and the Balkans. They finally stopped their advance just beyond the Adriatic Sea. If it had not been for the deaths of a few members of the Khan family, all of Western Europe might very well have fallen to this Eastern nomadic power.[40]

Genghis Khan, also known as *Temuchin* before he became ruler of the empire, was the son of a chieftain named *Esugal*. As a young man, Temuchin was known for his courage and shrewdness. After he finally managed to organize all of the Mongol tribes, Temuchin was given the name "Genghis Khan," which means "Supreme Ruler."[41]

After taking control of China, Persia and Khwarazm within just a few years, Genghis Khan fell ill and died in 1227. His empire was left to the Khan's four sons, who were called the "Golden or Sacred Kin." The Mongols reached deep into China and took Beijing in 1215.[42] By 1230, the Mongol empire controlled most of Central Asia from the Caspian Sea to Korea, and from Siberia to inside the borders of China and Persia.[43]

The Mongol soldiers were mostly very skillful horsemen. Conquering a great deal of territory was much easier on horseback, as long as there were no mountains or rivers in their way. Under Genghis Khan's two sons, Jochi and Batu Khan, the pair captured a stretch of land from Mongolia to much of Eastern Europe—a land that is sometimes called "The Steppe," a tall, grassy plain with flat land and temperate temperatures.[44] These days, that land is often referred to as the "Eurasian steppe."[45]

The first significant incursion into Kievan Rus' began in 1236 when Batu Khan led his forces into the Volga Valley and what today would be Bulgaria. Ports along the Volga were key trade routes for the Eastern Slavic peoples. Batu Khan's army soon came to be called the "Golden Horde." The Volga was the first significant river crossed by the Mongols. Next was the Dnieper River, three hundred miles west, where the city of Kiev could be found.[46]

About a century after the Golden Horde was formed, it rapidly began to collapse. Suffering from political fragmentation in the early fourteenth century, the Horde faced many internal struggles that peaked in a crisis in 1360. Because of these internal struggles, the Mongols began to afford unparallel autonomy to the princes of the Rus'. By the mid-fifteenth century, however, the Golden Horde was finally crippled beyond repair, and it disintegrated as quickly as it had begun two centuries earlier.[47]

One of the reasons that the Golden Horde came to an end was because of the death of their great leader, Ogedei Khan, in 1241. Another reason for the Mongol collapse was how difficult it had become for news in the empire to travel from one place to a distant place.[48]

Ogedei Khan, son of Genghis Khan

A third reason for the collapse of the Golden Horde was the expense that the Mongols had to go to in maintaining their large numbers of horses that gave them a military advantage. When things got bad for them in Central Europe, they turned their attention again to the East, where they pit their sites on the Song Dynasty in China, which they eventually conquered during the time of Kublai Khan.

Nevertheless, Europe, in general, and Russia, in particular, were not entirely absent of the influence of the Mongols. One of these ramifications was the division of the Eastern Slavic people into three separate nations—Russia, Ukraine and Belarus.[49] Another effect of the Mongol invasion was the rise of the Grand Duchy of Moscow, which began its independence from the Mongols in 1480. This duchy, of course, would eventually grow into the tsardom, or czardom of Russia. This is also the year of the Great Standoff on the Ugra River on October 4 of that year.[50]

The Great Standoff on the Ugra River was between the forces of Akhmat Khan, a leader of the Golden Horde, and the Grand Prince Ivan III of Russia. The standoff resulted in the retreat of the Tartars and is often taken as a sign that by 1480, the Mongols were pretty much finished with the Russians by then. We will say more about the czardom and the czars in Russia in the third section of this second part of this essay on the relation of Russia to Ukraine.[51]

This brings us to the second section of Part Two, in which we shall discuss another attempt to dominate Russia in the Interim Period, this time the Polish and Lithuanians in the sixteenth century.[52]

Polish and Lithuanian Invasion: Sixteenth Century

By the mid-fourteenth century, the lands that would become Ukrainian territories were under the leadership of three separate powers—the Mongol Golden Horde, the Grand Duchy of Lithuania, and the Kingdom of Poland. The Steppe and Crimea had coastal towns and their maritime traders were now in the hands of merchants from Venice and Genoa in Italy.[53]

By the mid-fifteenth century, the Golden Horde was in the process of being accepted by the Mongols. One of its successes were the Crimean Khanate that after the suzerainty of the Sultans of the Ottoman

Empire that had control of the Crimean Peninsula and large areas of the adjoining steppe.[54]

The Mongol rule over Ukrainian was largely indirect. The taxes and tributes were collected by local princes. The Grand Duchy of Moscow and the Grand Duchy of Lithuania had fought each other since the reign of Gediminas of Lithuania (1275–1341). Indeed, he may have been the founder of the Lithuanian empire. By the end of the fourteenth century, the duke of Lithuania had made the country one of the richest and most powerful in Europe.[55]

Gediminas began a series of wars between Lithuania-Poland and the Russian tsars. By the end of the fourteenth century, Lithuania-Poland had controlled vast stretches of East European lands from Kiev to Mozhaysk, a center for trade in the Moscow district. By this time, Lithuania and Poland had formed a partnership to fight the Russians more easily. What followed was a series of five Muscovite-Polish Lithuanian wars.[56]

Gediminas of Lithuania

The initial incursion of Polish-Lithuanian troops into the Principality of Moscow began in 1363. Five years later, General Algirdas of Lithuania (1296–1377) undertook the first great European expedition of Moscow. On November 21, 1368, Algirdas and his soldiers routed the sentry troops on the River Trosna, a small tributary of the Volga. However, he was unable to secure control of the Kremlin, the Russian word for "fortress" or "Citadel."[57]

The word "Kremlin" was first used in the fourteenth century. The structures of the contemporary Kremlin today date from the fifteenth century. Prince Ivan the Great (1440–1505) erected a structure that would rival the city of Constantinople. In fact, Ivan called his dream construction the Third Rome. He brought architects from Italy. Most of their work in Russia can still be seen today.[58]

At the beginning of the eighteenth century, the capital of Russia moved to Saint Petersburg, and the Kremlin was no longer the residence of the czars. Later, however, Moscow again became the capital during the time of Lenin and Stalin and the Russian Revolution.

Ivan III considered himself the heir to the fallen Byzantine Empire, as well as a defender of the Russian Orthodox faith. He proclaimed himself the "Ruler over All of Rus', and he proclaimed a connection between himself and Vladimir I of Russia. Moscow extended its influence to the Principality of Ryazan in 1456 and annexed the Novgorod Republic in 1477. Next was the Principality of Tver in 1483.[59]

However, there was also a series of disputes over border lines, mainly in the upper regions between Lithuania and Russia, mostly in the upper areas of the Oka River. Clashes broke out in these border wars.

At the end of the fifteenth century, Alexander, Grand Duke of Lithuania, sent a delegation to Moscow to negotiate a peace treaty signed on February 5, 1494. This was also around the time when Lithuania lost its first significant territory to the Russians. It was mostly the territory called Vyazma. The estimated loss was an area of approximately 87,000 kilometers, or 34,000 square miles.

The Third Muscovite-Lithuanian War took place in 1507 and 1508. Lithuania sent envoys to Moscow requesting the return of territory taken in the Second Muscovite-Lithuanian War of 1503. The new Lithuanian leader was Sigismund I. In December of 1512, the Moscow Principality invaded the Grand Duchy of Lithuania, mostly looking to recover the city of Smolensk. Fighting was fierce between the two sides, but the city finally fell in July 1514.

Sigismund had defeated the grand master and began to form associations with Kazan and the Tartar Hordes of the Crimea region. In 1522, another treaty called for a five-year truce. The same treaty was extended to 1534 after the first five-year pact. Vasily, the Emperor of Russia, died in 1533 when his son Ivan IV was only four years old. Consequently, his mother, Elena, acted as the ruler of Russia.

Sigismund I

Finally, in 1526 the Grand Duke of Moscow officially began to be called the "Tzardom of Russia," much like Ivan IV's claim to be "King over all Rus'." In this Interim Period, we have shown so far that the territory of the Kievan Rus' had been subjected to onslaughts, first by the Mongol Horde in the thirteenth century and then by the Polish-Lithuanian confederation in the sixteenth century.

This brings us to the final section of this second part of this essay, in which we will describe and discuss the early years of the Russian tsars.

The Early Years of the Russian Czars

The third element of this Interim Period we have been sketching out, we will now speak considerably about the rise of the czars in Russia and the roles they played in Russia-Ukraine relations. This section will bring us up to the Modern Age of these relations in the twentieth and twenty-first centuries.[60]

This third aspect of the Interim Period is concerned with two points. First, the annexation of Ukraine by Russia, and second, an analysis of the roles played by the Russian czars in Russia-Ukraine relations.

In 1793, the second partition of Poland under Russian rule of Empress Catherine II (the Great) of Russia brought the Right Bank of Ukraine into the Russian Empire. Earlier in the century, Kiev managed to abolish the tariff barriers between Russia and Ukraine, and the land of Ukraine began to grow commercially. Empress Catherine was fully aware of the importance of farmland in and around Kiev.

During the nineteenth century, Russia began to see Ukraine as economically important, particularly in the export of grain. In many places, the modern factory industry appeared, and Ukraine was known for its lumber mills and the building of ships.

For much of the history from the Middle Ages to the early twentieth century, Russia began to be ruled by a central monarch under the title of czar. Even before the use of this word in Russia and Ukraine, there was the title of "Grand Prince of Russia" held by Vladimir I and other Russian monarchs. The role of czar was a main staple of the Russian government from 1538 until 1917 and the Russian Revolution.

The Russian term *czar* is a derivative noun of the Roman name Caesar and the late Byzantine Empire. The Russian monarchs created the title to show that Russia—particularly Moscow, the capital—would become a "Third Rome" after the first real Rome in Italy and then the Byzantine capital of Constantinople, now modern-day Istanbul. There are other derivatives, such as czarista and czarina.

By the time of Peter the Great, the title czar began to be discarded and replaced with "Emperor of all of Russia." The name czar continued to be used until the overthrow of the monarchy in 1917. The use of the word czar was at its highest during the reign of Ivan IV, also called "Ivan the Terrible" (1530–1584). Some say he was the very first czar. Also, during his reign, the modern nation of Russia did not exist.

After the time of Ivan, Russia entered into what some historians call the "Time of Trouble." This was a period of political turmoil and out of that turmoil rose the Romanov dynasty, which ruled Russia until the end of the czarist period in 1917. The founder of this dynasty was Michael Romanov (1613–1645). The most successful of the Romanov czars was known as Peter the Great (1682–1721.)[61]

Ivan the Terrible, 1897. Artist: Viktor Mikhailovich Vasnetsov.
Oil on canvas, 97.2 x 51.9 inches. Tretyakov Gallery, Russia.

Peter the Great, 1717. Artist: Jean-Marc Nattier. Oil on canvas, 56.1 x 43.4 inches. State Hermitage Museum, St. Petersburg, Russia.

Altogether there were eighteen Romanov czars and czarinas. Fourteen of these were men and four were women—Catherine I (1725–1727), Anna (1730–1740), Elizabeth (1741–1762), and Catherine the Great (1762–1796), the longest reigning female leader.

The fourteen male czars included the following in their times of reign.

Michael Romanov (1613–1645)
Alexis I (1646–1676)
Feodor III (1676–1682)
Ivan V (1682–1696)
Peter the Great (1682–1725)
Peter II (1727–1730)
Ivan VI (1740–1741)
Peter III (Jan. 1762–July 1762)
Paul I (1796–1801)
Alexander I (1801–1825)
Nicholas I (1825–1855)
Alexander II (1855–1881)
Alexander III (1881–1894)
Nicholas II (1894–1917)

It was during Nicholas II's time that the czardom suffered political upheaval known as the Time of Trouble. It was out of this turmoil that the Russian Revolution arose. This brings us to the conclusions of Part Two. In Part Three to follow, we will speak of the period from the Russian Revolution up to the time of World War II.

The Russian expression, "Smutnoye Vremya," or "Time of Trouble," was a period of political struggle in Russia that followed the demise of the Rurik dynasty in 1598 and ended with the establishment of the Romanov dynasty in 1613. The period was known for foreign intervention, as we have shown by the Polish-Lithuanian Federation, as well as peasant uprisings and many attempts of pretenders to seize the throne and to threaten the destruction of the Russian state itself.

The Time of Trouble in the late sixteenth and early seventeenth centuries saw major social and economic disruptions, particularly in the southern and central portions of the Russian Empire.

The period began with the death of the last Rurik czar, Fyodor, in 1598. He was succeeded by his brother-in-law, Boris Godunov, who was faced in the Time of Trouble with an enormous famine from 1601 to 1603.

Portrait of Grand Duke Peter Fedorovich (future Peter III) and his wife Grand Duchess Catherine Alexeevna (future Catherine II), ca. 1745, artist: Georg Cristoph Grooth. Oil on canvas, 49.8 x 39.3 inches. Odesa Art Museum, Ukraine.

Conclusions to Part Two

We have devoted the second part of this essay on the history of Russia-Ukraine to sketching out what we have called the "Interim Period" regarding that history. This interim period, as we have shown, consisted of three parts. The first of these was the invasion of Kievan Rus' by the Eastern power, the Mongols. This invasion began in the early thirteenth century and continued well into the fifteenth century.

In the second portion of the second part of this essay, we described and discussed the attempts in the sixteenth century of the Polish-Lithuanian Commonwealth to take control of many portions of Russia, Ukraine and Moldova. These initial attempts on the part of the Polish-Lithuanian confederation occurred in 1363 and continued well into the sixteenth century.

In the third portion of Part Two, we indicated two principal goals. First, we explored the Russian annexation of most of Ukraine in 1793. Indeed, at that time—as in the time of Vladimir I—most Russians began to see the lands of Ukraine as part of Russia. This 1793 annexation clearly is one of the arguments of Vladimir Putin to bolster his view that "Russia and Ukraine are one people," as we will show more in Parts Five and Six of this essay.

The other principal goal of this section has been the development and a description of the phenomenon of the czardom of Russia—a series of Russian leaders from the sixteenth century and Michael Romanov, all the way to Czar Nicholas II, who was czar of Russia when the czardom was abolished during the Russian Revolution in 1917.

We have also shown in the third portion of Part Two that not all of the czars during the Romanov dynasty were men. In fact, as we have shown, four of the most important czars or czarinas of Russia were women. These were Catherine I, Anna, Elizabeth I, and Catherine the Great, who was the longest female monarch of the Russian Empire, ruling from 1762 until 1796. Catherine, however, called herself "Empress," what she saw as the female form of emperor.[62]

This brings us to Part Three of this essay on the history of the relations between Russia to Ukraine. In this third part, we will explore the period from the Russian Revolution in 1917 until the end of World War II in 1945.

Vladimir Lenin, 1920

Part Three
The Russian Revolution to the end of World War II

The Russian people are suffering from economic fatigue and from disillusionment with the Allies. The world thinks the Russian Revolution is at the end. Do not be mistaken. The Russian Revolution is just beginning.

—Alexander Kerensky

The Russians have proved that their only aim is really the improvement of the lot of the Russian people.

—Albert Einstein

Einstein's only failing was an unfortunate fondness for Josef Stalin and the Soviet Nation.

—Christopher Hitchens

Introduction

The Russian Revolution proved to be one of the most consequential events in the twentieth century. It inspired Socialist and Communist movements and revolutions throughout the world and continues to do so in places like Venezuela and Cuba. This part of the essay on the historical relationship of Russia to Ukraine will sketch out the causes and the events of the Russian Revolution in 1917, as well as the activities consequent from that revolution leading up until the end of World War II.[63]

What roles, for example, did Lenin and Stalin play in what would become the "Soviet Union?" How did the period in Russia from 1917 until 1945 help us understand Russia's relationship with Ukraine after the declaration of Ukraine's independence in 1991?

Causes and Events of the Russian Revolution

We will begin with what we consider to be the seven main causes for why the Russian Revolution began. We will list these seven causes here and then speak of each one at a time. Later in this section of Part Three, we also will give a summary of the major events in the Russian Revolution.[64]

The seven causes we have in mind are the following:

1. Defeat in World War I
2. Economic collapse
3. Dissatisfaction with the czar
4. The role of Czarina Alexandra.
5. The influence of the Industrial Revolution on Russia and Ukraine.
6. Rasputin.
7. The rise of the Bolsheviks.[65]

Russia entered World War I as a relatively underdeveloped nation. Although it had taken many significant steps forward in the twenty years before the war, Russia was far less industrialized than its allies in the war. Russia's navy had been nearly destroyed during a conflict with Japan between 1904 and 1905.

Revolutionaries protesting in Russia, February 1917

When Russia entered the war, General Alexander Samsonov was given command of the Russian Second Army for the purpose of invading East Prussia. He advanced slowly and had some initial successes, but by August 22, 1914, the Second Army was surrounded by the Germans.

General Samsonov attempted a retreat with no success. The Battle of Tannenberg lasted three days. Only 10,000 of the 150,000 Russian troops had survived. By December 1914, the Second Army had 6,553 combat troops but only 4,652 rifles. Untrained troops were drafted into the army, and by 1916, one-third of all Russian able-bodied men were in the army.[66]

Alexander Vasilevich Samsonov

By 1916, the czar and his generals realized that the Second Army could not sustain its participation, so Russia withdrew from the Great War. The involvement of Russia in World War I, however, had lasting consequences for the nation, its czar and his subjects, as well.[67]

For one thing, there were food shortages brought on by inflation. The food problem was not production; rather, it was distribution, for there was no organized system for feeding the Russian people.

In many ways, the Great War proved to be the death knell of the czarist empire. The transportation system collapsed as a consequence of the war. The Russian Army began to lose faith in the czar. Inflation, food shortages and the lack of public transportation brought widespread dissent from the Russian people.

In the second half of the nineteenth century, there was a population explosion in Russia. This greatly increased the need for food. Small Russian farmers, however, lacked modern equipment like tractors and other farm equipment, so they relied on traditional methods in their growing of food.[68]

After Russian farming became industrialized, the country became the largest producer of food in the world. Ukraine had gone through a similar lack of farming equipment and also became one of the largest producers of grain in the world to the point of being known as the "breadbasket of the world."[69]

Czarina Alexandra was never very popular with the Russian people. The chief reason for this is that she was German-born and was thought to be a German spy by many Russians at the time. Alexandra was the daughter of a Hessian duke and a granddaughter through her mother's side of Queen Victoria of Great Britain. Czar Nicholas II, therefore, was technically Alexandra's second cousin. Her demeanor was nervous and aloof, and her public behavior was often mistaken for coldness and arrogance. This led to further dissatisfaction among the Russian people before the revolution.[70]

Czar Nicholas II, 1912

Czarina Alexandra, 1908

The figure of Grigori Rasputin (1869–1916) is sometimes pointed to as a cause of the Russian Revolution. But he could have played no role in the Revolution, for he died a year before it began. There was, however, another revolution twelve years earlier before the one in 1917 before Rasputin came to the capital, and both occurred because the only Russian people who were happy with the czar and his family were the nobles.[71]

As indicated earlier in this section, most Russians were overworked, underfed and oppressed by the czarist regime. The Revolution was about the mistreatment and the dissatisfaction of the Russian people. In 1905, Rasputin, who was considered a mystic and fortune teller, predicted the collapse of the czarist empire, and many Russians firmly believed that prediction.[72]

At the end of his life, Rasputin came to exert some influence over Alexandra, particularly after Czar Nicholas left the palace during World War I to take direct control of the Russian Army. Some reports of the mystic in Russian pubs at the time say that the Siberian preacher openly boasted that the czarina, the throne, and the Russian government "were in his hands."[73]

This, of course, created some fodder for the scandal sheets of the Russian press, as well as the Russian Socialist propagandists. There were rumors of a sexual relationship between Alexandra and Rasputin when one of his letters leaked to the press. One paragraph said:

I kiss your hands and lay my head upon your blessed shoulders.[74]

A letter she wrote back included the line, "All I want is to sleep, sleep forever on your shoulder in your gentle embrace."[75] Before the czar left for the war, he asked his wife to take care of domestic affairs in his absence. For many, this was a grave mistake. The German-born queen was already the object of many rumors, one of which suggested that she kept a radio transmitter under her bed so she could communicate directly with the German kaiser.

Rasputin

Finally, the seventh and last cause of the Russian Revolution has to do with the rise of the Bolsheviks, our next topic for discussion in this first section of this essay in a historical context.[76]

On August 11, 1903, the Russian Social Democratic Labor party was formed. They met for their Second Party Congress in London in a chapel on Tottenham Court. At that meeting, the members took a vote. The result split the party into two factions. The first of these was called the Mensheviks, from a Russian word meaning "Minority." The other faction was the "Bolsheviks," from the Russian noun *Bolshinstvo*, meaning "majority." Vladimir Lenin led the Bolshevik party. His party did not gain the majority in Russia until 1922.[77]

This split in the party resulted in questions about who could join the party. Lenin was of the view that the party was to be a vanguard of those committed to a proletariat-based revolution—a revolution of the people. The new movement was particularly strong among the young in Russia.

The new Communist Party gained some traction in an event known simply as "Bloody Sunday" on January 22, 1905. On that day, an Orthodox priest led a protest in St. Petersburg. The czar's troops fired upon unarmed demonstrators. Two hundred people were killed, and eight hundred were wounded. Czar Nicholas would never regain the trust of his people after that day.

The Party was able to ride on the subsequent waves of popular anger against the czar and his regime. By October of 1917, the Party had established its manifesto, roughly based on the *Communist Manifesto* written by Karl Marx and Frederick Engels in 1848. Both of these documents emphasized the importance of class struggle in every historical society. The 1848 document also sketched out the many weaknesses it saw in the Capitalist economic system.

Karl Marx, 1875

Russia adopted the Communist system after the Russian Revolution. In fact, when the czar was dethroned in 1917, Vladimir Lenin returned to Russia after having been exiled for fomenting anti-czarist plots. Other Russian revolutionaries, like Leon Trotsky, for example, also returned to Russia to help with the new effort there.[78]

Leon Trotsky

Lenin promised the Russian people "Bread, Land, and Peace." He also authorized the beginning of what was called the "Red Terror," an execution order of former government officials under the czar, as well as members of the royal family.

Shortly thereafter, the country dissolved into a civil war between the Bolsheviks and what was called the White Guard, a loose alliance of anti-Bolshevik parties including the czarists, right-wing Russian nationalists, and anti-Communists. Both sides engaged in terror tactics that included executions and the establishment of prisoners of war camps.[79]

In 1921, Lenin established the New Economic Policy allowing for private businesses and a market economy, despite the fact that these went directly against Karl Marx's views on private property.[80]

Around the same time, Lenin annexed Armenia, Georgia, and then Azerbaijan in order to give the new government political and geographical protection. Vladimir Lenin died in January of 1924 of a heart attack.[81] After his death, several members of his Politburo vied for control of another new government. The winner of those scuffles was Josef Stalin, a key military member of the Red Terror. Stalin was also the general who led the 1921 invasion of Georgia, Stalin's homeland.[82]

Over the next several years, Stalin isolated his major opponents in the party, eventually throwing them out. He went on to become the unchallenged leader of the Soviet Union and was the official head of the Soviet Union from 1924 until 1953, when he died. One question that can be raised about this period is when exactly was Ukraine considered to be part of Russia and subsequently part of the Soviet Union?[83]

There are several ways these questions can be answered. It is clear that the majority of Ukraine was incorporated into the Russian Empire after the second partition of Poland in 1793. We will remember that before then, the Polish-Lithuanian Commonwealth held the right bank of Ukraine, while the left bank had been incorporated into the czardom of Russia.[84]

A second way to answer our questions is to say that in 1922, Ukraine became one of the original constituent republics of the Soviet Union during the time of Vladimir Lenin. Ukraine would not receive its independence again until the dissolution of the Soviet Union in 1991.

The years from 1944 to 1946 are another way to answer our questions. After the German-Soviet invasion of Poland in 1939, Lviv became part of the Soviet Union, and a few years later, from 1944 to 1946, there was a population exchange between Poland and Ukraine, each returning to the place and language of their origins.[85]

Finally, one may also answer our questions raised above with the year 1917 when the Ukrainian People's Republic proclaimed its independence. Thus, we may conclude that Ukraine was believed to be part of Russia and/or the Soviet Union in 1793, 1917, 1921–22, 1939, and 1944 to 1946.[86]

This brings us to the final task of this first portion of Part Three, in which we will sketch out the main events of the Russian Revolution of 1917. Many of which we already have mentioned in the analysis of this first section.[87]

Main Events of the Russian Revolution

We will suggest that the major events for understanding the timeline for the Russian Revolution go from 1887 until 1918. That timeline may be summarized this way:

> May 8, 1887: Lenin's brother, Alexander, is hanged for a plot to kill the czar.

> October 20, 1894: Czar Alexander III dies.

> November 14, 1894: Czar Nicholas II married Alexandra.

> December 8, 1895: Lenin arrested and sent to prison, then exiled.

> May 4, 1896: Nicholas II crowned czar.

> 1904: Alexandra gives birth to a son after four girls.

> January 9, 1905: Bloody Sunday in St. Petersburg.

> July 15, 1914: World War I begins.

> September 5, 1915: Nicholas II assumes control of the Russian Army.

December 17, 1916: Rasputin is murdered.

March 2, 1917: Nicholas abdicates, and his brother refuses the throne.

April 3, 1917: Lenin returns from exile.

July 3-7, 1917: Protests in Petrograd.

October 25, 1917: The Bolsheviks take over Petrograd.

October 26, 1917: The Bolsheviks take the Winter Palace.

February 1, 1918: The Bolsheviks changed from the Julian to Gregorian calendar.

March 3, 1918: The Treaty of Brest is signed between Germany and Russia, who leaves World War I.

March 8, 1918: The Bolsheviks changed the party name to the Communist Party.

March 11, 1918: The capital is moved to Moscow.

June 1918: Russian civil war begins.

July 17, 1918: Czar Nicholas II and his family are executed.[88]

Most of these events are self-explanatory. The final portion of this third part of this essay is the role that Josef Stalin played in World War II, to which we turn next.

Stalin's Role in World War II

The first thing to understand about Josef Stalin's role in World War II is that in August of 1939, he freed Hitler from his fear of the possibility of fighting a war on two fronts. He did this by signing a pact of non-aggression with Germany. A month later, however, Hitler's forces attacked Poland, which precipitated the beginning of World War II. In 1940 and 1941, Stalin became more concerned about Germany when Hitler decided to attack the Soviet Union and bring them into a war on the Eastern Front.

Hitler had wanted to neutralize an existing mutual defense treaty between France and the Soviets and to ensure that the Soviet Union would stand by when Germany invaded its next target—Poland. The act had included secret plans to divide Poland into spheres of influence, with the Nazis controlling the western half of Poland and the Soviets the eastern half.[89]

On September 3, 1939, two days after the Nazis invaded Poland, France and Great Britain declared war on Germany. After eight months of a "phony war," Germany launched its *Blitzkrieg*, or "lightning war," through Western Europe. In the process, the Nazis captured Belgium, the Netherlands, Luxembourg, and a good part of France; and all of this in just six weeks, starting in May of 1940.[90]

When France was taken, only Great Britain remained standing against Germany in Western Europe. And Hitler's attention turned to the east. By the end of 1940, Hitler had issued an order to plan to conquer Ukraine so that it was in the hands of Aryans rather than the native Slavic population that Hitler viewed as racially inferior.

Adolf Hitler, 1938

Hitler's Directive 21 was his plan to invade the Soviet Union. The plan was code-named "Operation Barbarossa," after the powerful medieval Holy Roman Emperor, Frederick (1122–1190). Directive 21 planned to advance along a line north to south from the Port of Archangel to the Port of Astrakhan on the Volga River, near the Caspian Sea.[91]

The Port of Archangel is at the mouth of the Severnaya Dvina River, in the southeast corner of Dvina Bay. The port handled cargo and passengers in World War II, but more recently, it is employed to transport oil. Rafts are also used at Archangel to transport lumber when the bay is not frozen from November until May most years.[92]

Hitler hoped to repeat his successes in Western Europe. He thought a victory in Russia would come quickly. On June 22, 1941, Operation Barbarossa was finally launched. It was Germany's largest contingent force of the war, including nearly 80 percent of the German armed forces.[93]

Between August 1939 and June 1941, Josef Stalin refused to believe that Hitler was planning to attack the Soviet Union, so the German Army caught the Soviets by surprise. The Nazis employed a three-prong attack—one prong toward Leningrad in the north, another in the direction of Moscow in Central Russia, and a third toward Ukraine in the south. German tank divisions and the *Luftwaffe*, or Air Force, aided Germany in gaining an early advantage over poorly trained Soviet forces. In one day alone, the German Air Force managed to put one thousand Soviet aircraft out of commission.[94]

The Germans took millions of Soviet soldiers as prisoners; its forces initially moved very quickly. The armed SS death squads, or *Einsatzgruppen*, followed in the army's wake. It sought to find and kill many Soviet civilians, especially Soviet Jews. Hitler's orders authorized the killing of all enemy officers immediately upon capture.

Although the Nazis made territorial gains, they also experienced very heavy casualties. The Germans had overestimated the size of the Soviet Army, and by the end of August, with German tanks just two hundred miles from Moscow, Hitler ordered that the drive to the Russian capital be delayed and to turn instead toward Ukraine in the south.

Kiev fell to Germany by the end of September. Germany managed, with the aid of Finnish troops, to cut off the city of Leningrad from the rest of Russia but not capture the city itself. Instead, Hitler ordered his forces to starve Leningrad in a siege that lasted 872 days. In early October 1941, Hitler ordered the start of another battle strategy called "Operation Typhoon." The purpose of this operation was to redirect the Germans back toward Moscow. During the delay, however, the Soviets reinforced their strength in Moscow with a million troops and over a thousand new T-34 tanks.[95]

After some initial successes, the muddy roads of autumn—known as the Rasputista, or "quagmire season"—stalled the Germans outside of Moscow, where they encountered the much better Russian defenses.

In the middle of the next month—November of 1941—the German Panzer divisions tried one final attempt to encircle and capture Moscow. Reinforcements from Siberia, however, helped the Red Army to counter the attack. Then, the brutal winter weather came next. That had more consequences for the moving of German tanks and other equipment. Nevertheless, in December, the Soviets mounted a surprise counterattack, putting the Nazis on the defensive and forcing them into a final retreat.

Needless to say, Operation Barbarossa was a dismal failure. Its main objective—to get Stalin to capitulate to the Nazis—was not an achievable goal. But the fighting was not over on the Eastern Front. Hitler ordered another strategic offensive against the Soviets in June of 1942 and in the Battle of Stalingrad in 1943. The victory at Stalingrad helped to turn the tide of the war in favor of the Allies.[96]

It should be clear that Josef Stalin's greatest accomplishment was his help in the defeat of Nazi Germany. Without Stalin's unique personality, tyranny, and unwillingness to employ draconian means of compulsion to compel his people to fight on, were great strengths of the Soviet leader. Many other countries surely would have given up with leaders of inferior skills.

Nevertheless, he was responsible for at least twenty million deaths. He achieved his plan to industrialize Russia and achieved power and status for Russia after World War II. He was nominated for the Noble Peace Prize twice in 1945 and 1948 but did not win either time. In two different years, *Time* magazine named Josef Stalin "Man of the Year."[97]

There is a wide variety of estimates of how many human deaths Josef Stalin was responsible for. A recent article by Kaleena Fraga, published on May 13, 2022, says the following about the matter, "After taking power in the 1920s, Joseph Stalin killed at least 9 million people through mass murder, forced labor, and famine, but the true figure may be as high as 60 million."[98]

This brings us to the conclusions of Part Three. In Part Four of this essay to follow, we will speak of Russian-Ukraine relations from 1945 with the end of World War II until 1991, when Ukraine declared its independence.

Lenin and Stalin, September 1922

Conclusions To Part Three

We divided the third part of this essay on Russian-Ukrainian relations from the Russian Revolution to World War II into three sections. In the first of these, we explored the major causes and components of the Russian Revolution. We sketched out what we see as seven major causes for why the Russian Revolution transpired from 1917 until 1922.

Some of these seven causes are political in nature, such as the rise of the Bolsheviks, while others were more historical, like the Russian defeat in World War I, the economic collapse of Russia in the 1880s and 1890s, and the widespread dissatisfaction with the czar among the Russian people before the Revolution.

Other contributors to the Russian Revolution, as we have indicated, also included the role of Czarina Alexandra prior to the Revolution, the influence of the Industrial Revolution in Russia beginning in the 1840s, and the figure of the mystic philosopher Grigori Rasputin, although he died a year before the Revolution began in 1916.

In the second section of this essay, we cataloged a timeline of events from the death of Lenin's brother in May of 1887 until the 1918 change by the Bolsheviks to the name of their organization to become the "Communist Party" on March 8, 1918.

The other events in our timeline included the January 1905 event known as "Bloody Sunday;" Czar Nicholas II's control of the Russian Army on September 5, 1915; the murder of Rasputin in December of 1916; and the Bolsheviks taking control of Petrograd in October of 1917 and the Winter Palace on October 26, 1917.

We also have emphasized in our Russian timeline Lenin's return from exile, the Bolsheviks changing the Russian calendar from Julian to the Gregorian calendar, and the Russian capital moving to Moscow in March of 1918. Needless to say, two other important events from that period were the start of the Russian civil war in June 1918, and the executions of Czar Nicholas II and his family on July 17, 1918, which were listed among the events in our timeline.

In the third and final section of Part Three, we sketched out and discussed at some length the major contributions Josef Stalin made to

Russian history from the Revolution in 1917 until World War II from 1940 to 1945.

In addition to the military decisions made by Stalin, we also commented on the relation of Stalin's Russia to Adolf Hitler and the Nazi Party. In fact, we emphasized that if not for the leadership of Josef Stalin, the Allies may not have won World War II.

In the close of section three, we emphasized what historians now call Hitler's "Directive 21," nicknamed "Operation Barbarossa." This was a play on the part of Hitler to attack the Soviet Union, beginning in the summer of 1941.

As has been true of most attempts to conquer Russia over the centuries, the chief hindrance to the invasion was the harsh weather and Russian topography. After some summer successes, the mussy roads of autumn literally stalled the German tanks outside of Moscow.

At the end of the third section, we pointed out the enigmatic views of Josef Stalin that, among other things, he was responsible for the deaths of at least twenty million people, while at the same time, he was nominated twice for the Noble Peace Prize and named twice as "Man of the Year" by *Time* magazine.

This brings us to Part Four of this essay on Russia-Ukraine relations. In this section, we will speak of the Cold War period, or roughly 1945, the end of World War II, until 1991, when Ukraine declared its national independence.

Russian President Boris Yeltsin announced his early resignation as head of state and the temporary transfer of his powers to Prime Minister Vladimir Putin, December 31, 1999.

Part Four
The Cold War: 1945 to 1991

Here's my strategy on the Cold War: we win, they lose.

—Ronald Reagan, May 29, 1988

Anti-Americanism may indeed have grown fiercer than it was during the Cold War. It is a common phenomenon that when the angels fail to deliver, the demons become more fearsome.

—Ian Burama, *A Matter of Principle*

Introduction

As we indicated in Part Three of this essay, the Soviet Union fought on the side of the United States in World War II, but relations between the two powers and their allies soon became strained after the war ended in 1945. The US and many of its allies were concerned about how powerful the Soviet Union was, as well as the nature of their Communist society and the view that all property is public and people share in the wealth that was created.

These concerns led to the Cold War, a long period of tensions between the United States and the Soviet Union that ended in 1991 when the Soviet Union broke up after many of its republics—such as Ukraine, Lithuania, and Estonia, for example—decided that they no longer wished to be Communist nations.[99]

After the Soviet Union dissolved in 1991, under the moderate Soviet President Mikhail Gorbachev, the former republics of the Soviet Union became fifteen independent states or nations. The largest and most powerful, of course, was Russia itself. Other nations included Ukraine, Lithuania, and Belarus and eleven other nations, as well.

During this time, Boris Yeltsin became president, and Russia went through many changes. Instead of the government being controlled by the Communist Party, people began to be elected to serve in representative democracies connected to newly formed political parties. Private businesses were now allowed to function. Individual citizens also had new political freedoms, including expressing themselves without fear of the government.

President Yeltsin was elected in 1996, but his poor health prevented him from serving his full term. He resigned a few years later, and he named Vladimir Putin as his Prime Minister to replace him as president.[100]

In 2000, Mr. Putin was formally elected by the citizens of Russia. In the first years of his presidency, he continued many of the strong-arm tactics of his predecessors. After the terrorist attack on September 11, 2001, Mr. Putin began to crack down on many of the new cultural freedoms and took control of the national television and radio networks. This, of course, allowed the government to greatly influence worldwide news reports about Russia.[101]

Mr. Putin was elected to a second term in 2004 but like in the US where you cannot serve more than two terms, Putin appointed his aide Dmitry Medvedev to serve as a proxy prime minister in 1998. It was clear, however, that Mr. Putin was still in charge.

In 2012, Vladimir Putin ran again for the Russian presidency and easily won. He was not, however, popular among the Russian people. The same year, many Russians protested the outcomes of local elections, mostly won by Putin candidates. Putin's police arrested many of the protestors and called them traitors.[102]

In 2014, Putin's troops invaded the Crimean Peninsula, an area of land in southern Ukraine that is bordered by the Black Sea. Mr. Putin maintained that the people of Crimea voted for independence from Ukraine.

Many people from Ukraine and leaders from several other nations did not like Putin's plan and believed the election in Crimea was a sham. In March 2014, however, Putin signed a "treaty" with some

Crimean leaders that said that Crimea was part of Russia. This was not surprising given the fact that Mr. Putin was born and raised in Crimea.

Many officials of Ukraine refused to recognize the annexation of Crimea and still considered the peninsula to be part of Ukraine, not Russia. After 2014, the Russian army remained on the peninsula of Crimea. Clashes broke out between Ukrainian rebels and Russian-backed supporters, who wished for all of Ukraine to be reunited with Russia.

In 2019, comedian and actor Volodymyr Zelensky was elected president of Ukraine. He ran on a platform that wanted to unite the country and end border battles with Russia over eastern Ukraine. To help in their cause, the United States pledged to give millions of military aid to help fight the Russian occupation of eastern Ukraine.[103]

In July 2018, President Donald Trump was accused of withholding these funds from Ukraine unless they investigated Trump's political rival, Joe Biden. Zelensky refused, and Mr. Trump was later impeached by the House of Representatives.[104]

Volodymyr Zelensky, August 26, 2019

In February 2022, Mr. Putin announced the invasion of Ukraine and sent Russian troops to take over the major cities of Ukraine, including the capital Kiev. Since that time, the war in Ukraine has gone on.

In this fourth part of this essay on the relations of Russia with Ukraine, our principal purpose is to discuss what we see as the six periods of what has come to be called the Cold War from 1945 until 1991. This is the focus of the next section of Part Four.

History of the Cold War: 1945 to 1991

What we have labeled the Cold War can be explained by the relationships between the world's two superpowers in the four decades following World War II. In that time, six different periods of the Cold War can be described. We will list these six here and then discuss them one at a time consecutively.

These six periods and the years they occurred may be summarized in the following way:

> 1945 to1947: End of World War II and Post-War Activities
> 1947 to 1953: Containment and the Truman Doctrine
> 1953 to 1962: Crisis and Escalation
> 1962 to 1979: Confrontation to Détente
> 1979 to 1985: The New Cold War
> 1985 to 1991: The Final Years[105]

In the first phase of the Cold War listed above, immediately after the end of World War II, the United States and its allies created the NATO military alliance in 1949 in the apprehension of possible Soviet attacks into Europe. The global policy that followed from 1947 to 1953 was called "Containment," in that the West wanted no more territory taken by the USSR.

The "Truman Doctrine" was an American foreign policy initiative whose main goal was "containing" the Soviet geopolitical expansion during the Cold War. The doctrine was announced to Congress in March of 1947 and was further developed in July of 1948 when Mr. Truman pledged to contain Communist uprisings in Greece and Turkey.[106]

This containment period, from 1947 until 1953, saw the beginning of the Iron Curtain, the Marshall Plan, the Berlin Blockade and Airlift, and German rearmament. It was also a time when China had a civil war, and the US was engaged in the Korean War.[107]

The former occurred when the Southeast Asian Treaty Organization was formed in 1955. It was created by Southeast Asian nations who worried about Communist influences there. The new Communist government in China, of course, was in favor of that expansion. Other Chinese rebels were not.[108]

The Soviets responded to NATO in 1955 by forming the "Warsaw Pact," which was officially called the "Treaty of Friendship, Cooperation, and Mutual Assistance." The treaty was signed in Warsaw, Poland, in May of 1955, by the Soviet Union and seven other Eastern Bloc nations. It was created as an attempt to make a balance of power or counterweight to NATO.[109]

The period called "Crisis and Escalation" from 1953 until 1962 saw a number of important events and movements, including Khrushchev's rise to power and the de-Stalinization process, the signing of the Warsaw Pact, the Space Race, the crisis in Berlin, and what is now called the Cuban Missile Crisis, followed by the ousting of Khrushchev.[110]

The "Confrontation to Détente" period from 1962 until 1979 saw the United States involved in the Vietnam War, the French withdraw from NATO military structures,[111] and Richard Nixon and Russian General Secretary Brezhnev enter the two superpowers in a period of what was called "Détente." This was a time of easing Cold War tensions between the US and the Soviets, from 1967 until 1979. It was a time for increased trade, the opening up of China to the US, and the signing of the SALT treaties, or Strategic Arms Limitation Talks.[112]

The "New Cold War" period was characterized by the Soviets' war in Afghanistan and Ronald Reagan and Margaret Thatcher as heads of state in America and Britain. It was also the time of the Polish solidarity movement and the eventual withdrawal of Russia from Afghanistan a decade after its original incursion.[113]

There was no direct military action between the two organizations. The conflict between the two was entirely ideological in nature and sometimes through proxy wars. The largest military incursion on the part of the Warsaw Pact was the direct invasion of Czechoslovakia in August of 1968. All of the pact nations participated, except Romania and Albania. In fact, Albania withdrew from the pact a month after the action in Czechoslovakia.[114]

The Warsaw Pact began to unravel further with the spread of revolutions in 1989, starting with the solidarity movement in Poland and its electoral success in June of 1989. East Germany withdrew from the pact in 1990. Finally, on February 25, 1991, at a meeting in Budapest, Hungary, the Warsaw Pact was dissolved by its six remaining states.[115]

The Soviet Union was also dissolved in late December 1991, although many of the former Soviet Republics formed an organization called the "Collective Security Treaty Organization" shortly thereafter in early 1992.[116]

In the following two decades, many of the Warsaw Pact nations joined NATO, but not Russia. East Germany unified with West Germany and joined NATO. The Czech Republic and Slovakia soon followed, as did many of the Baltic States that earlier had been part of the Soviet Union.

In the sixth and final period of the Cold War—from 1985 until 1991, when the Soviet Union was dissolved—there was a thaw in relations between the two great superpowers. President Gorbachev introduced many political and social reforms, and many of the Eastern Bloc nations broke away from the dominance of Russia and the Soviet Union.[117]

In addition to the main reasons for the collapse of the Soviet Union we have mentioned here, there are at least eight other contributing causes to the dissolution of the Soviet Union. We will list these factors here and then discuss them individually. These factors may be summarized this way:

1. Changes in leadership.
2. Ethnic and linguistic tensions.
3. Demographic catastrophes.
4. The war in Afghanistan.
5. Proxy wars around the world.
6. Growing unpopularity in Central and Eastern Europe. Public realization of discontent and dysfunction with economic and social structures.

7. Proliferation of production of whistle-blowing and anti-regime documents.[118]

Regarding item number one above, when the Soviet leadership went from Brezhnev to Andropov, then Chernenko, and then to Gorbachev, these men had vastly different views about the Stalinist-Leninist doctrine, so that they became increasingly disconnected from the original Communist/Socialist goals of the Soviet Union.

Many ethnic and linguistic tensions arose among Soviet states, particularly between the Russian-speaking regime leaders and many of the ethnic enclaves and non-Russian-speaking portions of the Soviet Union, what might be called the "Hinterlands."

There were also many demographic changes that occurred in the Soviet states. For example, a lack of incentives to have children ultimately led to a rampant level of abortion in the Soviet states.

Concerning item number four in the above list, one effect of the Soviet war in Afghanistan that lasted for ten years was the hemorrhaging of blood and treasure in Afghanistan. Soviet soldiers often turned to hard drugs to ease the tensions and the military backwardness of the Soviet army.

Another clear factor in the collapse of the Soviet Union was the number of proxy wars that occurred around the world from the late 1970s on. These proxy wars could be seen, for example, in places like Nicaragua, El Salvador, Angola, Mozambique, Yemen, Namibia and many other locations throughout the world.

The growing tensions among other states in Central and Eastern Europe with the Soviet Union in the late 1980s and early 1990s also contributed greatly to the collapse of the Soviet Union. This was particularly true, for example, among those participants in Poland's solidarity movement. That spirit soon spread to Czechoslovakia and many other nations of Central and Eastern Europe.

The seventh factor on our list is the public dissatisfaction in the 1980s and early 1990s with the economic and social systems of the Soviet Union. This was particularly true after the introduction of the ideas of *Glasnost* and *Perestroika* across the many Soviet states.

Finally, in the 1980s and early 1990s—before the collapse of the Soviet Union—there was a proliferation of new media and technology to more easily reproduce documents related to the local Soviet state rebellions. For example, photocopy machines and cell phones began being used to mass produce copies of whistleblowing and anti-Soviet regime documents and became more readily available to the average Soviet citizen and his family.

Thus, with this new analysis, we now have eleven separate factors that we believe went into the collapse of the Soviet Union from July of 1991 until Christmas Day of the same year when the Soviet flag was lowered for the final time at the Kremlin.

This brings us to the second section of Part Four of this essay, in which we will discuss the phenomenon of the dissolution of the Soviet Union, our next topic for discussion on the relations of Russia and Ukraine.

Dissolution of the Soviet Union: 1988 to 1991

On the morning of December 25, 1991, the Soviet flag flew over the Kremlin in Moscow for the final time. The representatives of several Soviet Republics, including eleven in all, had already announced that they would no longer be part of the Soviet Union. This included Ukraine.

The three Baltic republics—Latvia, Lithuania and Estonia—also declared their independence from the USSR. Only one of the former Soviet Republics remained—Kazakhstan. Although the republic did not officially withdraw from the USSR, there were anti-Soviet activities in Kazakhstan going back to 1986, when three thousand citizens protested the appointment of Gorbachev-backed Gennady Kolbin, an ethnic Russian, to be president there.

In 1989, Kazakh's parliament passed an ordinance that the official language was now Kazakh, and Russian was to be used for government communications. In 1990, the Supreme Soviet in Kazakhstan elected Nursultan Nazarbayev, the first ethnic president. He was elected on October 25. Finally, in August of 1991, the new president condemned an attempted anti-Gorbachev coup in Moscow and Kazakhstan, at the insistence of protestors, was forced to resign from the Communist Party and the Soviet Union and was the last state to go. By the late summer of 1991, all of the former Soviet republics were now independent states.[119]

The once-mighty Soviet Union had fallen, largely due to the greater number of radical reforms that Soviet President Gorbachev had implemented during his six years of leadership of the USSR. Gorbachev himself, however, was gravely disappointed in the break-up of the Soviet republics, so much so he resigned on Christmas day 1991.

This brings us to the second portion on the relations of Russia to Ukraine, where we will enumerate the reasons for the collapse of the Soviet Union at the end of 1991.

Main Reasons for the Collapse of the Soviet Union

From our perspective, there were five major reasons why the Soviet Union collapsed in late 1991. We will enumerate those reasons here and then speak about them individually.

These five main reasons were the following:

1. Perestroika and Glasnost
2. An Aging Politburo
3. Aggression from the West
4. Guns and Butter
5. Many Nationalist Movements[120]

The plan that President Gorbachev had for political openness and eliminating any final traces of Stalinist repression was certainly a significant cause of the collapse of the Soviet empire. Among those Stalinist touches was the eradication of the Russian Secret Police—the KGB. One way to see this phenomenon was the removal of a statue of Felix Dzerzhinsky taken down in Moscow in August 1991.[121]

Another big change from Stalin's day was that newspapers and television broadcasts could now criticize the government, and political parties other than the Communist Party could now participate in elections.

Perestroika was Gorbachev's plan for the economic restructuring of the Soviet Union. He wanted to institute a hybrid economy, a kind of blend of Communism and Capitalism. The Politburo would still control the direction of the economy while allowing market pressures to dictate some production and distribution decisions.[122]

But by loosening controls over the Soviet people and making these changes to the political and economic systems there, the Soviet government appeared weak and vulnerable. The Soviet people used their newfound freedoms often to protest the government, and in late 1991 they successfully ended Soviet rule.

Secondly, the Soviet Union founders, for the most part, were driven by ideological purity that was fundamentally tied to Marxism. That kind of commitment did not continue in the following generations among the Soviet people.

The removal of Nikita Khrushchev from office in 1963 signaled a fundamental change in Soviet policies. The Politburo began to move farther and farther away from the visions of Lenin and Stalin.

The 1960s and 1970s saw a rapid increase in the wealth and power of the Communist Party elite. While average Soviet citizens died from starvation, Politburo members enjoyed luxuries like rich people in the West. The younger generation saw this and refused to buy into the party ideology.

At the same time, throughout the 1980s, the Soviet government was subject to harsh criticisms from the West. In a speech before the British House of Commons on June 8, 1982, President Ronald Reagan called the Soviet government an "evil empire."

Reagan's leadership also led to massive increases in American military spending, as well as new research into new and more efficient weapons. The United States also isolated the Soviet Union from the global economy, and this helped to drive down prices of oil and other commodities.

Without the oil revenues to which they were accustomed, these aggressive gestures from the West helped to bring the Soviet economy to a crumble. If we add the fact that the Soviets also had to spend a fortune to keep up with the West in the arms race, the Soviet economy was doomed.

Regarding our fourth major reason for the collapse of the Soviet Union—that is, guns and butter—every economy has a limited number of resources with which they may make goods (guns) or consumer goods (butter) for a nation's economy. If a nation over-emphasizes guns, the people are left without the butter. On the other hand, if a nation focuses too much on butter, there often are not enough resources to grow the economic capacity of the nation, nor to protect it.

Concerning the economy, Josef Stalin had a series of five-year plans, starting in 1928 to 1932 and continuing to his fifth plan from 1950 until 1955. He did not live to see these plans come to fruition, for he died in 1953. Curiously enough, Stalin's successors continued the practice of economic five-year plans, all the way to the twelfth plan from 1986 until 1990.[123]

Josef Stalin's five-year plans, however, were almost entirely driven by a need to produce strategic goods for the Soviet Union. The Soviets funneled all its available resources directly into industrialization, so they could compete with the rest of the world. Many economic shortages undermined the argument that the Soviet political system was superior to Capitalism. Thus, the Soviet people began to call out for change and a revolution.

Finally, in regard to "Many Nationalist Movements," the Soviet Union was composed of fifteen radically different republics. Across individual nations, there were dozens of ethnicities, languages and cultures, many of which were incomprehensible to each other. Much bullying of ethnic minorities took place in the 1980s by the Russian majority. This created many tensions among the people in outlying regions of the Soviet Union.

As a result, by the late 1980s, nationalist movements in Eastern Europe brought many regime changes. In 1989, there was a great change in Poland.[124] This movement soon spread to Czechoslovakia, to Yugoslavia, and to many other Soviet satellites in Eastern Europe. As these Soviet republics began to pull away from the Soviet Union, the power of the central government was greatly weakened.

This brings us to the third and final section of Part Four of this essay on Russia-Ukraine relations in which we will discuss the final days of the Soviet Union from August of 1991 until Christmas Day of that same year.

Final Days of the Soviet Union

The beginning of the last days of the Soviet Union can be traced back to March 1991, when the USSR held a referendum on whether the union should be preserved or dissolved. More than three-quarters of Soviet citizens wanted the union to survive, but six republics abstained from voting on the issue at all.[125]

Five months later, on August 18, 1991, Communist hard-liners in the government and the military had seen enough. They placed President Gorbachev under arrest at his vacation villa in Crimea. The rebels said that the president had "an inability to serve due to health reasons." He could no longer fulfill his presidential duties.[126]

The leaders of the coup then declared a state of emergency. On August 19, 1991, tanks rumbled throughout Moscow as thousands of Soviet citizens poured into the streets. They linked hands in human chains and built barricades to protect the Russian parliament, known as the White House. Outside the parliament, Yeltsin rallied the crowds, speaking from atop a tank. But the popular uprising was doomed, and the coup was a failure after only three days.

President Gorbachev flew back to Moscow on August 22, 1991, but he did not become a hero in the end. That place was reserved for Yeltsin. By that time, Yeltsin had already taken control of the KGB. Left with no choice, the Yeltsin contingent wrote a speech to be delivered by Mr. Gorbachev. It was delivered on December 25, 1991.[127]

In that address, Mr. Gorbachev said:

We are now living in a new world. An end has been put to the Cold War and to the arms race, as well as to the mad militarization of this country, which has crippled our economy, public attitudes, and morals...The old system collapsed before the new one had time to begin working.

A few paragraphs later, Mr. Gorbachev added:

Fate had it that when I found myself at the head of the state, it was already clear that things were not well in the country. There is plenty of everything: land, oil and gas, other natural riches; and God gave us lots of intelligence and talent, yet we lived much worse than other developed countries and keep falling behind them more and more.

At the close of the Christmas speech, Mr. Gorbachev ended with these words:

> I am leaving my post with apprehension, but also with hope, with faith in you, your wisdom and force of spirit. We are the heirs of a great civilization, and its rebirth into a new, modern and dignified life that now depends on one and all. Some mistakes surely could have been avoided, many things could have been done better, but I am convinced that sooner or later our common efforts will bear fruit, our nations will live in prosperous and democratic society. I wish all the best to all of you.

Moments after this Christmas speech, Mr. Gorbachev signed over the Soviet nuclear codes into the hands of Boris Yeltsin. Then, without pomp and circumstance, the red flag of the Soviet Union was lowered on the Kremlin's main flagpole. The Soviet Union was sixty-nine years old at its death.

This brings us to the conclusions of Part Four of this essay. This will be followed by the fifth and final section on Russia-Ukraine relations, in which we will discuss the contemporary period of that relationship from 1991 to the present.

Conclusions to Part Four

Part Four of this essay has been devoted to the phenomenon known as the "Cold War Period." To that end, we divided it into three separate sections. After some introductory comments, we turned our attention to an explication of the history of the Cold War.

In that initial section of Part Four, we divided the history of the Cold War into six periods from 1945 to 1991 called the End of World War II and Post-War Activities; Containment and the Truman Doctrine; Crisis and Escalation; Confrontation to Détente; The New Cold War; and The Final Years. We also discussed many major events in each of these six periods.

In the second section of Part Four, we set forth what we claimed to be the five principal causes of the collapse of the Soviet Union. The five reasons we enumerated and discussed were the following:

1. The Phenomena of Perestroika and Glasnost
2. An Aging Politburo
3. Aggression and Tensions from the West
4. What we called "Guns and Butter"
5. And the many Nationalists Movements and Revolutions in the sixteen Soviet Republics

We have also shown in this section how each of these separate factors greatly contributed to the fall of the Soviet Union, both politically and economically and in terms of the many Soviet social structures. Mr. Gorbachev's plans for openness and the elimination of any traces of Stalin-era repressions were at the heart of Gorbachev's efforts.

In the third section of Part Four, we concentrated our attention on what we labeled "The Final Days of the Soviet Union," a time that went from March of 1991 until Christmas Day of the same year when President Gorbachev of the Soviet Union resigned and Boris Yeltsin took over the government. It also saw the lowering of the Soviet flag at the Kremlin in Moscow for the final time.

Most of the facts during these ten months are not in dispute, but it was a time by which most of the fifteen republics of the union had resigned, and many of the traditional political systems among the Soviets had been altered or abandoned, such as the KGB, or the Secret Police of the Soviet Union and the government-controlled newspapers of the Soviet states.

We also indicated that the "sickness and incapacity" of Mr. Gorbachev at his vacation villa in Crimea had a staged and orchestrated character to it. For the most part, even the Christmas resignation speech he delivered appeared to have been written by someone else. Thus, in a real way, Boris Yeltsin and his crew seem to have had the final word on the eighty-year-old Soviet Union.

This brings us to the fifth part of the essay. In this section, we will explore and discuss what we shall call the "Vladimir Putin Era," the time of contemporary Russian-Ukrainian relations from 1991 until the present war in 2022.

Vladimir Putin in his KGB uniform, ca. 1980

Part Five
Vladimir Putin and His War in Ukraine

I would rather try something great and fail than to do nothing and succeed.

—President Vladimir Putin

The truth of the matter, you saw what happened in Bucha, this warrants him, he is a war criminal. This guy is brutal, and what's happening in Bucha is outrageous and everyone's seen it.

—President Joe Biden

Introduction

In the fifth part of this essay, we have the following goals. First, to introduce and discuss the person of Russian President Vladimir Putin, his history and biographical information.

In the second section, we will raise the question, "Why does Putin want Ukraine?" At the same time, pointing out what we see as the major causes of the 2022 Russian war in neighboring Ukraine. What does he hope to gain from the war, and how successful is he likely to be?

In the third and final section, we will raise the question about the possible resolutions to the war in Ukraine, as well as how this war may come to a close. Needless to say, the answer to that question at this point is a murky one. But we will, nevertheless, end this essay with some observations that may be helpful in understanding a possible and final resolution.

The Life and Times of Vladimir Putin

Vladimir Vladimirovich Putin was born on October 7, 1952, near Leningrad, Russia, now called St. Petersburg. He studied law at the Leningrad State University, where his favorite tutor was Anatoly Sobchak, later one of the leading politicians in the Perestroika period.[128] Vladimir Putin served fifteen years as a foreign intelligence officer for the KGB, or Committee for State Security, including six years in Dresden in what was then East Germany, as an intelligence officer.[129]

In 1990, Mr. Putin retired from the KGB with the rank of Lieutenant Colonel. He then returned to St. Petersburg, where he became prorector of the Leningrad State University.[130] His responsibilities in that post were to be in charge of what was called "external relations," specifically, matters outside of Russia. At that time, Mr. Putin also became an assistant to Mr. Sobchak, his university tutor.

Not long after this, in the city of St. Petersburg, Mr. Sobchak became the first democratically elected mayor, and Mr. Putin continued to be one of the mayor's chief advisors. Putin was well-liked because of his ability to get things done. By 1994, he had become Mayor Sobchak's chief deputy.

Two years later, in 1996, Vladimir Putin moved to Moscow where he joined the presidential staff as a deputy to Pavel Borodin, the Kremlin's chief administrator at the time under President Boris Yeltsin.[131] On December 31, 1999, Mr. Yeltsin unexpectedly announced his resignation and at the same time, he named Vladimir Putin the new interim president.

A year later, in March 2000, Mr. Putin easily won the presidential election with 53 percent of the vote. As president, he sought to end corruption in Russia and to establish a strongly regulated market economy for the country. He also quickly reorganized Russia's eighty-nine regions and republics, dividing the country into seven federal districts, each headed by an administrator appointed by Mr. Putin.[132]

During his first term, the Russian economy grew under Putin on average by seven percent annually. He also saw a five-fold increase in the price of Russian oil and gas. He also led Russia against a group of Chechen separatists.

During his third term as president, Russia annexed Crimea and sponsored a war in Eastern Ukraine that required several military incursions with Russian troops.[133] Mr. Putin also ordered a military intervention in Syria against rebel and Jihadist groups.[134]

In September 2015, President Vladimir Putin ordered the Russian military to intervene on behalf of Syrian President Bashar al-Assad, who was in the midst of the fifth year of the Syrian civil war. Russia already had provided weapons to Syria. The Russian intervention helped to turn the war decisively in favor of the president.

In his fourth term as president, he presided over a military buildup on the border with Ukraine. Putin accused the Ukrainian government of committing atrocities. In April 2014, groups of unidentified gunmen outfitted with Russian equipment seized government buildings, mostly in southern Ukraine. This sparked an armed conflict between Kiev and Russia, but Mr. Putin steadfastly denied he was behind the fighting.

On July 17, 2014, Malaysia Airlines flight MH17, carrying 298 people, crashed in eastern Ukraine. Overwhelming evidence suggested that the plane was shot down by a Russian surface-to-air missile fired from a rebel-controlled area.[135]

Western countries responded with sanctions on Russia. Soon Russian oil and gas prices plummeted, sending the Russian economy into a tailspin. At the time, NATO officials estimated that more than a thousand Russian troops were actively fighting inside Ukraine. Soon Russian and Ukrainian officials met for cease-fire talks in Minsk, Belarus, on September 5, 2014. The signed cease-fire had no effect.[136]

On February 12, 2015, Mr. Putin met with other world leaders in Minsk to approve a twelve-point peace plan aimed at ending the fighting in Ukraine. The fighting ceased for a while, but by September 2015, the United Nations estimated that some eight thousand people were killed in Ukraine and another 1.5 million had been displaced.[137]

On September 28, 2015, in an address before the United Nations, Mr. Putin presented his vision of Russia as a world power. Two days later, Russia became an active participant in the Syrian civil war when Russian planes struck targets near the cities of Homs and Hama. These attacks seemed to be aimed at the opponents of Russian ally and Syrian President Bashar al-Assad.[138]

Mr. Putin's designs on Ukraine did not end there. On February 24, 2022, the Russian government launched a massive attack on Ukraine. Their initial thought was to depose the government and to keep Ukraine from joining NATO. As we shall see in the next section, however, Mr. Putin abandoned the idea of conquering Kiev.[139]

Putin and the War in Ukraine: 2022

The initial goal of Vladimir Putin regarding Ukraine was to overrun the country and to depose its government in Kiev. A second original goal was to keep them from joining the Western defensive alliance, NATO. After a month of fighting in the capital, however, and a month of failures, Putin abandoned his bid to capture Kiev and instead turned his attention toward the east and south of Ukraine.

When the Russian invasion of Ukraine was announced on February 24, 2022, Mr. Putin mentioned two goals. First, to demilitarize and de-Nazify Ukraine. Second, the Russian president announced his desire that Ukraine continue in its neutral status regarding NATO.[140]

The first charge against Ukraine, regarding the Nazis, goes back to World War II when Stepan Bandera led a Ukrainian insurgent army, whose men killed thousands of Jews and Poles, including many women and children. At the same time, Bandra's army fought alongside the Nazis against the Red Army and Communism.[141]

After the war, many of Stepan Bandera's followers remained in Ukraine. After the 2014 incursion of Russia into Crimea, the number of Bandera admirers and other collaborators has dramatically increased. Mr. Putin's comment about the de-Nazification of Ukraine is directly related to the Bandera movement.[142]

President Putin was not alone in his Nazi claim about Ukraine. In early March 2022, the Russian foreign minister accused Western countries of ignoring what he called war crimes in Ukraine, saying that their silence "encouraged the on-set of Neo-Nazism and Russophobia."[143]

Foreign Minister Sergey Lavrov and Russian intelligence chief Sergei Naryshkin joined the fray. The former said that Ukraine was "being released from foreign oppression," while the latter observed that "Russia's future and its future place in the world are at stake."[144]

At the time of the February invasion, Ukraine's democratically elected President Volodymyr Zelensky told Ukrainian reporters, "The enemy has designated me as enemy number one. My family is target number two."[145] A top advisor of Mr. Zelensky said at the time that "Russian troops made two separate attempts to enter and control the presidential compound.[146]

In a speech on April 17, 2022, President Putin spoke of the invasion as a "noble cause." Russian leaders refuse to call it a war. Instead, they preferred to call it a "special military operation." The claims of Nazis in Ukraine are carried over from the post-World War II era when some prominent Ukrainians cooperated with the Nazi government, and Mr. Putin believes that this influence still exists in the government of Ukraine.

This becomes extremely unlikely, however, when we consider that President Zelensky is Jewish and the grandson of a Holocaust survivor. In fact, at the beginning of the invasion, February 27, 2022, Zelensky told the London *Times*, "I was raised in a normal, Soviet Jewish family." Today, Ukraine is the only state outside of Israel to have both a Jewish head of state and a Jewish head of government. In the February interview, Mr. Zelensky asked, "How could I be a Nazi? Explain that to my grandfather."

Nevertheless, a month into the invasion of Ukraine, Russia pulled back from Kiev and declared that its main goal was now the "liberation of Donbas," an area of Ukraine that broadly refers to the eastern Ukraine regions of Luhansk and Donetsk. Russia already controlled about a third of these regions in the 2014 proxy war in Ukraine.[147]

If the Russians do capture Luhansk and Donetsk, it is likely that Putin will annex them, followed by a sham vote, as he did in 2014 in Crimea. So the "war" goes on, and Russia will most likely turn its attention to the south of Ukraine, followed by annexation and a popular, pro-Russia vote. By this point, Ukraine would officially again be part of the Russian Federation.

This brings us to the second section of Part Five, where we will describe and discuss the three main causes of the Russian invasion of Ukraine that began in late February 2022. In other words, why does Putin want Ukraine to be part of the Russian Empire?

Why Does Vladimir Putin Want Ukraine?

We have raised the question here why Mr. Putin and his followers want Ukraine to be part of Russia. What are the causes of the current hostilities in Ukraine? To that question, we may point to at least three principal answers. We will list these three here and then discuss each of them individually.

1. Historical reason
2. Ukraine and NATO
3. Russian prestige and restoring an empire[148]

Regarding our first reason for Putin's invasion of Ukraine, with the 1991 break-up of the Soviet Union, Russia lost control of the fourteen former republics it had dominated, but the loss of Ukraine was the most bitter of those republics.

As shown in Part One of this essay, the two countries have been linked since the ninth century when Kiev became the capital of the ancient Russian state of Kievan Rus'. Then, the leader of the Rus' kingdom, Vladimir I (980–1015), introduced Orthodox Christianity to Russia. From 1654, Russia and Ukraine were united by a treaty under the reign of the Russian czars.[149]

President Putin alluded to this historical connection in June of 2022, in the fourth month of the war, when he said, "We are one people who share a single, historical and spiritual space." He also commented that "What now appears like a wall between the two is tragic." Kiev rejected his argument as being politically motivated and an oversimplification of history.

Regarding Russia-Ukraine and NATO, since the Cold War ended, NATO has expanded toward the east by taking fourteen new members, including many of the nations of the Warsaw Pact and the three Baltic nations that the Soviet Union once controlled. These are Lithuania, Estonia and Latvia. Russia saw this as an encroachment of its borders.[150]

Now Ukraine has a vision of joining NATO. It is not yet a member, but it has a promise from 2008 that it will eventually get to join. Since Ukraine toppled a pro-Russian president in 2014, it has moved ever-increasingly closer to the West, including the staging of joint military operations with NATO troops.[151]

NATO has also taken delivery of weapons, including US Javelin anti-tank missiles, as well as drones from Turkey. To help in the Ukrainian cause, Kiev and Washington have more cooperation than at any other time since the collapse of the Soviet Union.

Washington has been particularly helpful to Ukraine after Russia seized the Crimea region in 2014. But Russia still backs groups of separatists in Ukraine who are still fighting government forces in eastern Ukraine. Mr. Putin believes that Ukraine's growing ties with America and the NATO alliance are a danger to the continued well-being of Russia.

Mr. Putin's reason for this fear is that he knows that the charter of NATO explicitly says, "Any attack on any member is an attack on all of NATO." If Ukraine were to become a member of the Western alliance, then any incursion into Ukraine would be seen as a war against all the member nations. And clearly, the Russian president would not want that.[152]

The third reason we have mentioned for why Russia has moved into Ukraine has to do with the prestige that Russia now has with the rest of the world, as well as Mr. Putin's apparent desire to reconstitute some version of a new Russian empire. During the Cold War, the Soviet Union was one of the two great superpowers, and its place in geopolitics has been sufficiently diminished.

In fact, when the Soviet Union collapsed in December 1991, Vladimir Putin called the Soviet fall "The greatest geopolitical catastrophe of the twentieth century."[153] In December 2021, he called the independence of former Soviet states a "major humanitarian tragedy."[154] President Putin wants Russia to still have an exalted place in the world, whether the rest of the world thinks so or not.

Thus, it would appear that Russia and Mr. Putin have invaded Ukraine for three main reasons. These are historical reasons, his desire to keep Ukraine out of NATO and his desire to regain a lofty place in the geopolitical world scheme, a place that Mr. Putin believes Russia deserves.

It is also clear that there are many other reasons in addition to these three discussed here about why Russia invaded Ukraine. Consider, for example, that Mr. Putin waited until Joe Biden became the American president so that Donald Trump was no longer in office. This timing seems not to be an accident. The lack of confidence that the American people have in Mr. Biden most likely also goes into the machinations of the Russian president.[155]

Similarly, Mr. Biden's blaming of high energy and food prices on Mr. Putin's war fed right into the Russian president's desire to be somebody in the world once again. What better way to do that than to damage the United States? Meanwhile, the inflation Biden blames on Putin began long before the invasion of Ukraine, going all the way back to the first day of Biden's administration when he canceled the Keystone Pipeline, among his other acts to discourage the use of fossil fuels.[156]

But this raises yet another question about the Russian war in Ukraine and can be put quite simply. "Is there a way out of the war in Ukraine?" This is the topic of the third section of Part Five of this essay.

Is There a Way Out of the War in Ukraine?

Normally, the way to resolve an international event like the war in Ukraine is to negotiate to find a resolution. In this case, however, there is little sign of any negotiated activity to end the war in the immediate future. There were some attempts at negotiation early in the war, back in March, but there has been nothing since then.

At the end of April, President Putin told the United Nations secretary-general, "We are negotiating, we do not reject talks." But earlier that same month, he declared negotiations about the war to be "at a dead end."

In an effort to help things along, Austrian Chancellor Karl Nehammer met with Putin and then, on April 16, 2022, gave a very pessimistic assessment of a man who has "entered into a logic of war." Meanwhile, on March 16, 2022, President Zelensky quietly accepted that Ukraine would not soon join NATO. "It's a truth," he said recently, "and it must be recognized."

After atrocities came to light in Bucha, Mariupol, and elsewhere, President Zelensky made it clear that there would be no more talks until Russia withdrew all its troops from all territory seized since February 24, 2022.

On March 28, 2022, a month after the war began, Kiev put forward a five-point plan, an "offer of neutrality," to end the war in Ukraine. These five points may be summarized in the following way:

First, Ukraine would become a non-aligned and non-nuclear state, with no foreign military bases or contingents on its territories.

Second, Ukraine would be given strict, legally binding guarantees requiring other countries to protect a neutral Ukraine in the event of attack.

Third, within three days, guarantor states would have to hold consultations and come to the defense of Ukraine.

Fourth, Ukraine would be allowed to join the European Union (EU) but would not enter into military-political alliances nor any international exercises that would require consent from guarantor stats.

And finally, the future status of Russian annexed Crimea would be negotiated over the next fifteen years.

This plan, of course, is heavy on the defense of Ukraine. It says nothing, however, about negotiating parts of Ukraine that may become parts of Russia in the future.

In that regard, some scholars are suggesting that the Donbas Region should be given to Russia in exchange for the immediate end of all hostilities in Ukraine. One only wonders, however, how long it would be before Russia wants more of Ukraine, particularly the capital of Kiev and territories in the southwest.

The five-point plan does mention Crimea, but with the proviso that its status would be negotiated in the future. One final question that can be raised about Vladimir Putin and his war in Ukraine is whether the Russian president has any designs beyond the acquisition of the nation of Ukraine. This is the topic for the fourth section of Part Five of this essay.

Does Putin Have Designs Beyond Ukraine?

If Vladimir Putin has any designs beyond the acquisition of Ukraine, the military setbacks incurred by Russia so far in the war certainly have put a damper on any larger designs beyond the borders of Russia and Ukraine. The most immediate threat is that of the Republic of Moldova, a nation that is not a member of NATO.

It is clear that Russia's invasion of Ukraine in late February 2022 sent shock waves across all of Europe but nowhere stronger than in neighboring Moldova, one of the poorest nations in all of Europe. Moldova has long sought to balance its relationships with Russia with western Moldova taking in more refugees from Ukraine than any other European nation. The war also has spurred officials in the capital of Moldova, Chisinau, to ask for membership in the European Union.

The nation of Moldova, however, is completely dependent on Russia for its supplies of gas and oil, so they have held off on joining the Western sanctions that the US and others have placed on Russia.

In April, the acting commander of Russia's Central Military District, Rustam Minnekaev, said that one of the goals of Russia's renewed interest in Ukraine is to create a corridor to Moldova's Russian-backed separatists' enclave in Trans-Dniester—a sliver of land between Moldova and Ukraine.[157] On April 27, 2022, two months after the start of the war in Ukraine, Commander Minnekaev said, "This would be to prevent the oppression of the Russian-speaking population in Moldova."

Of course, once Russia established its proxies and separatist movement in a foreign land, the next step historically has been an election that quickly brings the separatist group to power, followed by a later announcement that the new land is now part of the Russian Federation. As we have indicated earlier, this was the three-step plan for Russia to take over Crimea in 2014.

In light of the struggles that have beset the Russian military in Ukraine so far, most political analysts are skeptical that Moscow will push further west along the Ukrainian coast to the Trans-Dniester that hugs the eastern flank of Moldova.

Meanwhile, Russia has taken a hit with Finland and Sweden desiring to join the NATO alliance that now seems as unified as ever. At the beginning of the war, Mr. Putin revealed his ambition to roll back the NATO membership to pre-2000 But with the war in Ukraine, the Russian president's desire has appeared to have the opposite effect.

Regarding Moldova and its dependence on Russian oil, President Putin has already punished two other NATO members—Poland and Bulgaria—for the West's support for Ukraine, simply by cutting off their gasoline supplies.[158]

Six weeks after the start of the war in Ukraine, US President Joe Biden labeled Mr. Putin a "war criminal." He also told reporters that "We are collecting evidence to support war crime charge against Mr. Putin, while working on new charges and continuing to provide weapons to Ukraine's defense forces."

On February 27, around the same time as Mr. Biden's war criminal comments, German Chancellor Olaf Scholz said that "Putin wants to build a Russian Empire…He wants to fundamentally redefine the status quo within Europe in line with his own vision." If Mr. Scholz is correct, and if Moldova is next, that leads us to ask a final question: "After Moldova, what's next?"

One interesting fact about the plans of Mr. Putin consists of the desire for land, to organize a rebel separatist group, and hold elections and designate a proxy leader. This is the same plan we saw in the Crimea region, strikingly similar to how Josef Stalin incorporated many of the republics in the Soviet Union. Mr. Putin's strategy is not a new one. It has already been battle-tested.

This brings us to the conclusions of Part Five on Russian-Ukraine relations. This material will be followed by a section on the sources of this essay.

Conclusions to Part Five

We divided the fifth and final part of this essay on Russia-Ukraine relations into four distinctive parts. In the first of these, we have provided an outline and the career of Russian President Vladimir Putin. In that first section, we spoke of Mr. Putin's early life in St. Petersburg, as well as his education and subsequent career in his various military and political positions.

The second section was dedicated to what we see as the three main causes of Russia's war in Ukraine. We suggested that these causes went into the making of Putin's war in Ukraine.

We have labeled these:

1. For historical reasons.
2. For reasons related to Mr. Putin and the NATO Alliance.
3. Because Mr. Putin has a passion for restoring the place and prestige of Russia in world politics.

In the third section of Part Five, we raised the question, "Is there a way out of the war in Ukraine?" We were very pessimistic that the war in Ukraine would end anytime soon.

We also enumerated in this section a five-point plan, or "offer of neutrality," proposed by Kiev by which the war in Ukraine may be resolved. We showed that these five points were heavy on Ukraine's defense and short on negotiations and the switching of land in Ukraine to Russia, with the exception of Crimea.

In the fourth and final section of Part Five, we raised the question of whether Mr. Putin has designs on territories that go beyond the nation of Ukraine. In other words, is he looking to build a new Russian empire?

We also pointed out that the most likely next territory in the designs of Mr. Putin is that of Moldova, a non-NATO member, as well as one of the poorest nations in all of Europe. And that some comments from Rustam Minnekaev, the acting commander of Russia's Central Military District, would seem to support the view that Russia has some interests in the Trans-Dniester Region of Moldova, a piece of land between Ukraine and Moldova.

It may well be, then, that the proper understanding of the mind of President Vladimir Putin is that at the heart of his plans is the reconstitution of some kind of new Russian Empire that begins with Ukraine in 2022 and continues to its neighbor Moldova as many of its leaders believe, and then onto other former Soviet Union territories.

Finally, we have made two other points about Russia's interests in Ukraine and perhaps in other former Soviet republics, as well. First,

Russia has shown a pattern of invading the territories of other states that consists of a desire for acquisition, the support of rebel separatists in the desired land, and then the election to put Russia's proxy in charge.

The second point we made in section four is that President Putin did not invent the pattern mentioned above. Rather, he learned these steps from the political career of Josef Stalin when he was in the process in the 1930s to 1950s of acquiring republics for what became the Soviet Union.

The pagan Vladimir I chooses Christianity as the new State religion for the Kievan Rus in 987; Prince of Novgorod, Grand Prince of Kiev and ruler of Kievan Rus' from 980 to 1015. His father was prince Sviatoslav of the Rurik dynasty. Courtesy of Bridgeman Images.

Part Six
The Role of Religion in the Russia-Ukraine War

To promise to abide by this legislation, so inimical to God,
would mean forsaking the gospel and turning away from
God's law. This is why Christians have a choice to make, either
to trade in their loyalty to God for freedom from persecution,
or to remain true to Christ and consequently to run the risk of
persecution.

—Mikhail Khorev, *Letters from a Soviet Prison Camp*

Religion is the sigh of the oppressed creature, the heart of a
heartless world, just as it is the spirit of a spiritless situation.
It is the opiate of the people.

—Karl Marx, *Critique of Hegel's 'Philosophy of Right'*

And this is where the words of scriptures come to mind.
There is no other love rather than if someone gives soul for
their friends.

—Vladimir Putin, reference to the Gospel of John 15:13

Introduction

One final aspect for consideration regarding the causes of the 2022
war between Russia and Ukraine is the role that religion had played
in the Soviet Empire and subsequently in the relations between the
two countries since Christmas of 1991 when the Soviet Union was
dissolved.

In Part Six, we will begin with a short history of the place of religion in the Soviet Empire. This will be followed by a description of the three major faiths that continue to be practiced in Ukraine. In the third and final section, we will explore the roles that religion and discrimination may now play in the war between the Russian Federation and the country of Ukraine.

Religion in the Soviet Empire: Some History

As one of the founders of the Soviet Union, Vladimir Lenin referred to the idea of religion this way:

> Religion is the opiate of the people. This saying of Marx is the cornerstone of the entire ideology of Marxism about religion. All modern religions and churches, all and of every kind of religious organizations are always considered by Marxists as the organs of bourgeois reaction, used for the protection of the exploitation and the stupefaction of the working class.[159]

It is clear that what Marx and Lenin believed about religion is that it is a way of dulling people into avoiding one of the harshest realities of human life—that is, that there is no God. Indeed, in their view, the proper response to religion should be nothing more than Atheism. In fact, in another place, in commenting on Georg Hegel's *Philosophy of Right*, Marx told us:

> Religious distress is at the same time the expression of real distress and the protest against real distress. Religion is the sigh of the oppressed, the heart of a heartless world, just as it is the spirit of a spiritless situation. It is the opiate of the masses.[160]

For Marx and Lenin, then, religion is both a critique of religion and its replacement with atheism and a criticism of society itself, in particular, the use of religion by the upper classes to keep the lower classes in their economic places. Marx and Lenin suggested that religion is meant to create an illusory fantasy for the poor, a fantasy that is not true.

Thus, it is not surprising that the official Soviet view of religion from Vladimir Lenin on was a posture of atheism. This view can be seen as early as the first Russian Federation Constitution from July 10, 1918. Among the provisions of this document were the following:

1. No church or religious group could own property.
2. The church is to be considered separate from the state.
3. Monks and clergy of all denominations were forbidden to vote.[161]

The same document also states that: In government and all publicly administered buildings, without exception, are forbidden to,

1. Hold any religious functions or ceremonies (prayer services, funerals, etc.)
2. House any kind of religious items (icons, pictures, statues of a religious nature, etc.)[162]

The same constitution also included another nine provisos that were particularly aimed at wiping out the practice of religious faith in the Soviet Union. In fact, this became the general attitude of Josef Stalin toward religion, as well. From 1928 until 1941, the USSR conducted an anti-religious campaign. It began in 1929 with the passing of legislation that severely limited religious activity in order to disseminate atheism and materialism philosophy.

The main religious target of Stalin was the Russian Orthodox Church which had the largest number of faithful in the country. Nearly all of its clergy, as well as outstanding religious Soviet advocates, were shot or sent to labor camps. Theological schools and seminaries were closed, and church publications were prohibited. One report suggested that 85,000 Orthodox priests were shot in 1937 alone.[163]

The bottom line for religion in Josef Stalin's era was very simple: the Russian Orthodox Church, as well as the Orthodox and Catholic churches in Ukraine and in other Soviet states, were outlawed in the Soviet Union from 1946 until 1989. What is known as the Ruthenian Catholic Church, or the Carpatho-Rusyn Catholic Church, also began to be suppressed in 1949 and continued until Stalin's death on March 5, 1953.

This brings us to the second portion of Part Six, in which we will describe and discuss the three major faiths in the Soviet Union from the death of Stalin until the demise of the Soviet Union in late 1991.

Three Main Faiths in Soviet Union and Ukraine: 1953 to 1991

From the death of Josef Stalin until the collapse of the Soviet Union, both Russia and Ukraine had three principal faiths. These were the Russian Orthodox Church, the Ukrainian Orthodox Church, and the Ruthenian Catholic Church.

Catholics who live in Ukraine tend to reside in four southwestern oblasti, or subdivisions of Ukraine—Transcarpathia and three other districts: Lviv, lvano-Frankkivsk, and Ternopil. These are the districts that make up Galicia.

It was only in 1989 that the government of Ukraine began to allow the Ukrainian Catholic parishes to register with the government and begin to practice their faith openly, which had been suppressed for over forty years. The Ukrainian Catholic Church had lost some three thousand churches taken over by the Russian Orthodox Church due to the Synod of Lviv of 1946.

Not surprisingly, Ukrainian Catholics, with new-found religious freedom, wanted their churches back. During the time of President Gorbachev, his uses of glasnost and perestroika, for the most part, allowed more religious freedoms for those in the Ukrainian Catholic Church.

In 2014, after the Russian annexation of the Crimean Peninsula, Archbishop Gullickson, the Nuncio of Ukraine Catholics, immediately reported that "There is little doubt that Russian Orthodox hostilities and intolerance began to be practiced against Catholics in Ukraine."[164]

Thus, before Vladimir Putin took control of the Russian Federation in 1991, there were three main faiths in the Soviet Union and particularly in Russia and Ukraine. These were the Russian Orthodox Church, the Ukrainian Orthodox Church, and the Ruthenian or Catholic Church of Ukraine. All three of these faiths were suppressed from the 1940s until 1990. And some scholars suggest that the persecution of Catholics in the southwest of Ukraine has continued since President Putin took office. This brings us to Mr. Putin's views on religion and what role these views may have played at the beginning of the Russian invasion of Ukraine in February of 2022.

Putin on Religion and its Role in the War in Ukraine

To make sense of the views of President Vladimir Putin on religion, we must first summarize some relevant facts in understanding what role religious faith may have played as a cause of the war in Ukraine. These facts include the following:

1. President Putin grew up in Leningrad in the period of the Soviet Union when all religion was suppressed.
2. Thus, Mr. Putin must have learned and incorporated into his belief system Marx's dictum that "Religion is the opiate of the masses."
3. In several major speeches leading up to the invasion of Ukraine, President Putin has suggested what he has called a "spiritual union between Russia and Ukraine, principally in the figure of Prince Vladimir I of Kiev."
4. The Russian Orthodox Church in general, and Kirill, the patriarch of Moscow and primate of the Russian Orthodox Church, has been one of Mr. Putin's supporters in the war in Ukraine. In fact, he has offered what might be called a "spiritual cover" when he noted that the war is a "metaphysical struggle more than a physical struggle."[165]
5. Patriarch Kirill was a member of the Russian Orthodox Church that suppressed the exercise of other religions in the Soviet era. He was born in 1946 and was head of the Leningrad Church after attending seminary. Kirill was ordained on April 3, 1969. On December 6, 2008, Kirill became the Patriarch of Moscow.
6. Like Putin, Patriarch Kirill grew up in Leningrad and must have been exposed to the Marxist indoctrination, atheism and materialism of the Marxist-Leninist.

From this set of six facts, several questions arise about the views Putin and Kirill have about God. For example, how much did President Putin internalize the Marxist-Leninist views of atheism and materialism? How much did Mr. Putin experience the suppression of religion in his early adult years? When did President Putin begin to have his new "Spiritual Enlightenment?"

Similarly, we may also ask, How much did Patriarch Kirill internalize the doctrines of the Marxist-Leninists? How much did he participate in the suppression of other faiths besides that of the Russian Orthodox religion? And perhaps the most important question about the patriarch is, how does he reconcile his faith in Vladimir Putin and his faith in what the Russian Church calls God Almighty? Indeed, a similar question can be raised about the current president of the Russian Federation. How much of Putin's Marxist-Leninist past continues in the heart of the Russian leader? And how are those residing beliefs from Communism to be reconciled with his new-found theological views?

The answers to these questions, for the most part, are not clear. But it may well be the case that the Soviet era's suppression of religion, as well as the suppression of Catholics in southwest Ukraine, and the traditional view that religion is the opiate of the masses may be another factor that continues to contribute to Russia's war in Ukraine.

If Putin's plans involve the constitution of a New Russian Empire, as we have suggested earlier in this study, then the annexation of Ukraine, Belarus and Moldova, and maybe even beyond, might bring us back to a Soviet-like era reminiscent of Putin's greatest hero—Josef Stalin himself.

One might also, of course, ask what the true relationship is between Kirill and Putin. Is the patriarch a tool of the president or is he the chief spiritual advisor? The patriarch sometimes speaks of a vision he calls the Russkiy Mir, or "Russian World" in English. Is this the basis for Putin's war or simply the theological glaze applied to it?

How can a religious leader—and a Christian leader at that—who had any moral integrity support a war that is so brutal? And might another spiritual leader, Pope Francis, with whom Patriarch Kirill entered into a dialogue in 2016, persuade him to withdraw his support and urge Putin to have his troops stand down? Wouldn't that be a great end to this current war? It might be the best way for all parties involved to save their faces.

Meanwhile, the leaders of various religious organizations in the U.S. with some histories in the region have commented on the place of religion in contemporary Ukraine. Conferences held on Zoom and on "Public Orthodoxy," a website sponsored by the Orthodox Christian Studies Center at Fordham University, have both bitterly criticized Russia's role in Ukraine. In April of 2022 at a conference at Georgetown University, a Ukrainian Greek Catholic Archbishop named Borys Gudziak remarked about the state of religion in Ukraine:

> There are so many explicit expressions of intention that to our surprise are actually the results of us not wanting to hear—not hearing.[166]

Also, in April 2022, George Demacopoulos, a theologian at Fordham University who was honored as an Archon, or a "Distinguished Christian," by the Ecumenical Patriarch of Constantinople, Bartholomew I, declared that "Putin is an instrumentalizer of religion." What Professor Demacopoulos meant was that "Rather than looking to Putin's religion as a guide to action, Putin attacked Ukraine and then invoked Christianity to justify the invasion using the traditional Christian Just War Theory."[167]

Other theological critics of the Russian invasion of Ukraine with respect to the issue of religion are the Commission of Catholic Bishops of the EU who called upon Patriarch Kirill "to appeal to Russian authorities to immediately stop the hostilities against the Ukrainian people," and especially the Catholics in the southwest.[168] In the same letter, the Catholic bishops implied that the Catholic clergy in southwest Ukraine were being discriminated against by the Russian Federation.

The World Council of Churches (WCC), of which the Russian Orthodox Church has been a member since 1961, also wrote to Patriarch Kirill on March 2, 2022. The WCC asked for "mediation so that the war might be stopped." The letter added, "Raise up your voice on behalf of the suffering brothers and sisters, most of whom are faithful members of your Orthodox Church."[169]

In his response on March 10, 2022, the patriarch mostly employed Kremlin double-speak, suggesting that the war is a "struggle between the Russaya Mir, or 'Russian World,' and the West." Kirill said "Western forces had conspired to use Ukraine to make a brotherly people enemies." The patriarch added, "All Western efforts to integrate

Ukraine were founded upon a geopolitical strategy aimed at weakening Russia."[170]

Not all of the religious criticisms of the Putin-Kirill Holy War are foreign ones. Father Nikolay Platonov, for example, posted a YouTube video criticizing Patriarch Kirill for having "justified" the war and "blessing military action in Ukraine." The priest also dismissed the patriarch's comments that "gay parades in the Donbas" were the cause of much violence. Platonov called this "ridiculous."[171]

Father Platonov also noted that the Moscow Diocese had begun to put pressure on priests who were not in concert with the war, as well as some priests who outright refused to collect donations from parishioners to support the Russian Army in Ukraine. Father Platonov observed the following about these activities:

> No one asked the priests' opinions. All those who
> disagree are being identified—they will smear everyone.
> No one will be left out.[172]

At the end of his YouTube video, Father Platonov observed this about President Vladimir Putin:

> I say this to those who can still see and hear, who still have
> a conscience. Run...run. A crazy sub-human is in power who
> will retain power at any cost. On the altar of his vanity, he will
> lay hundreds of thousands of people—your children and the
> children of a neighboring state.[173]

In the city of St. Petersburg, several priests were arrested because they spoke out against the war in Ukraine. Another man was arrested in front of the St. Petersburg Cathedral because he carried a placard with the words from Psalm 34:14. This psalm tell us:

> Turn from Evil and do Good.
> Seek peace and pursue it.[174]

Russian Federation media watchdog, Roskomnadzor, also regularly blocks websites with information about the war. Some of the recently blocked materials include a Belarus media report on the destruction of churches in Ukraine and a Protestant pastor who appealed to fellow clergy in Russia to speak out against the war.[175]

There is no doubt that President Putin has used his Russian Orthodox faith as a way of supporting his invasion of Ukraine that began in February of 2022. He even used the traditional Just War Theory in his announcement right before the war. It is just as clear that the patriarch of the Russian Orthodox Church, Bishop Kirill, is Putin's number one cheerleader in the Russian military action towards its southern neighbor.

Both men appear to see the war as a "metaphysical struggle" between the Russian world and the forces of evil coming from the West. Most of the world's Christian critics of this perspective, such as the Catholic bishops and the World Council of Churches, see the war in Ukraine more on moral terms, with the religious believers of Ukraine being on the side of the good, while the Putin Administration and the Russian Orthodox Church are on the side of moral degradation.

This brings us to a discussion of the major conclusions made in this essay, followed by the major sources we have relied on in the construction of this essay.

Vladimir Putin, 2021

Part Seven
Some Conclusions of this Study

Only God can make an elephant out of a fly.

—Traditional Russian Proverb

Take these seeds and put them in your pockets. So, at least sunflowers will grow whenever you lie down in this place.

—Volodymyr Zelensky

Introduction

The purpose of this seventh part on Russia-Ukraine relations is to make some observations about the major conclusions made in it. We will accomplish this goal by making observations about each of the previous six parts, starting with Part One and continuing consecutively to Part Six.

We will achieve this task by speaking about each part in terms of the goals explicitly set forth at the beginning of the six parts, from Part One's emphases on Prince Vladimir and Kievan Rus' to Part Six: The Role of Religion in the Russia-Ukraine War.

Conclusions to Part One

The main goal of Part One was the introduction to Prince Vladimir I of Kiev, the progenitor of the empire known as Kievan Rus'. After some brief comments on the life of Vladimir and his family, we turned our attention to the religious conversion of Vladimir from his historical Nordic-Slavic polytheism to the Eastern Orthodox Church, centralized in Constantinople under the leadership of Basil II.

Another goal was to speak of the geographical extant of the Kievan Rus' that was at its widest extent around the middle of the eleventh century. This included significant parts of what today are Russia, Ukraine and Moldova.

A third goal was to describe and discuss the internal clashes among the sons of Vladimir and his grandsons. We have shown that ultimately one of his grandsons, named Yaroslav, was the winner of these struggles. Yaroslav was so influential, in fact, that he is called "Yaroslav, the Wise" by the Eastern Orthodox Church.

We also made some comments about President Vladimir Putin on the place of Prince Vladimir in the history of Russia and its people. In fact, the president of Russia recently suggested that Prince Vladimir was the "Moral Foundation of the Earliest Slavic Empire."

Lastly, in Part One, we made some remarks about the etymology of the place names of the early Slavic kingdom, as well as what Kievan Rus' was called by the Arabs, Greeks and Romans, and by the various Nordic peoples—Norway, Sweden, Finland and Denmark.

Above all, the major takeaway from Part One was the role of Prince Vladimir and the foundations and conversion of the Kievan Rus' empire that can be traced back to the tenth and twelfth centuries.

Conclusions to Part Two

We have referred to the second part of this essay on Russia-Ukraine Relations as the "Interim Period" consisting of three waves of Russian invasion, beginning in the thirteenth century. The first of these invasions came at the hands of the eastern power, the Mongols. This invasion, as we have shown, began in the early thirteenth century and continued well into the fifteenth century.

Most of the major Mongol leaders in this period were related to the family of the greatest Mongol leader, Genghis Khan (1162–1227). Other prominent members of the Khan clan included Ogedei Khan (1186–1241); Mongke Khan, who, between 1236 and 1242, attacked western Asia, Russia, Poland, and Hungary; and Batu Khan, among many others. We also introduced the Mongol leader Hulega Khan (1217–1265), a grandson of Genghis Khan, who invaded Persia and the Middle East between 1253 and 1259. He greatly expanded the southwestern portion of the Mongol Empire.

The second invasion of Russia in the interim period came in the sixteenth century at the hands of the Polish-Lithuanian Commonwealth. In fact, the commonwealth took over significant portions of Russia, Ukraine and Moldova. This Polish-Lithuanian incursion into Russia began in 1363 and continued well into the sixteenth century.

In the third incursion of the interim period, we sketched out the history of Russia's attempt in 1793 to annex Ukraine. Indeed, as we have pointed out, at the time of Vladimir I, most Russians had already seen Ukraine as part of Russia. In fact, this was one of the arguments that Vladimir Putin employed before the invasion of Ukraine, saying that "Russia and Ukraine are one people."

Another goal of part two of this essay has been an introduction and discussion of the phenomenon of the czardom of Russia, beginning in the sixteenth century with Czar Michael Romanov and going all the way to Czar Nicholas II who was the leader of Russia when the czardom was abolished during the Russian Revolution.

We also pointed out that not all of the czars during the Romanov dynasty were men. In fact, four of the most important Russian leaders were czarinas. They were Catherine I, Anna, Elizabeth I, and Catherine the Great, who ruled Russia from 1762 until 1796. Catherine the Great, however, called herself "empress," which she saw as the female version of emperor.

Conclusions to Part Three

The main focus of Part Three of this essay has been on the period in Russia from the Russian Revolution until the end of World War II. In this section, we had three principal goals. The first of these was a discussion of the major causes and components of the Russian Revolution.

In fact, we enumerated seven major reasons why the Russian Revolution transpired from 1917 until 1922. As we have shown, some of these seven reasons were political in nature, like the rise of the Bolsheviks, some were more historical, like Russia's defeat in

World War I, and some were economic, like the collapse of the Russian economy in the 1880s and 1890s.

Another contributing factor that went into the making of the Russian Revolution was the widespread dissatisfaction the Russian people had with the czar. Other contributing factors we discussed in Part Three concerning the Russian Revolution were the role of Czarina Alexandra prior to the Revolution, and the influence of the Industrial Revolution in Russia, beginning in the 1840s. We also indicated that mystic philosopher, Grigori Rasputin, may have played a role in the Revolution, though he died in 1916, a year before it began.

Another goal was to provide a catalog of major events from the death of Lenin's brother in May of 1887 until the 1918 change by the Bolsheviks of the name of their organization to become the "Communist Party." That change was made on March 8, 1918.

The other major events of our timeline included the January 1905 event known as "Bloody Sunday," Czar Nicholas II's decision to take over control of the Russian Army on September 5, 1915, the murder of Rasputin in December of 1916, and the Bolshevik takeover of Petrograd in October 1917 and the Winter Palace on October 26, 1917.

We also emphasized in our Russia timeline Lenin's return from exile on April 9, 1917, the Bolsheviks' change of the Russian calendar from Julian to Gregorian, and the moving of the Russian capital to Moscow in March 1918. Two other major events, of course, were the start of the Russian civil war and the executions of Czar Nicholas II and his family on July 17, 1918.

Another goal of Part Three was to sketch out at some length the major contributions that Josef Stalin made in Russian history from the end of the Revolution to the end of World War II in 1945.

In addition to Stalin's important military decisions, we also commented on Stalin's Russian relation to Adolf Hitler and the Nazi Party. In fact, we pointed out that without the leadership of Stalin, the Allies may not have been the victors in World War II.

We also discussed Hitler's Directive 21, nicknamed "Operation Barbarossa." This was a plan of the Nazis to invade the Soviet Union, beginning in the summer of 1941.

Like most of the other attempts to conquer Russia over the years, the major impediment for the Nazi army was the harsh weather coupled with the Russian topography. After some summer successes, the muddy roads of autumn stalled the German tanks outside of Moscow.

Finally, at the end of Part Three of this essay, we spoke about some of the paradoxes found in Josef Stalin. Not only was he responsible for the deaths of at least twenty-five million people, but he was also nominated twice for the Nobel Prize for peace and was named "Man of the Year" twice by *Time* magazine.

Conclusions to Part Four

Part Four of this essay has been devoted to the phenomenon known as the Cold War. To that end, we have had four main goals. The first of these was to provide a six-period timeline sketching out the history of the Cold War from 1945 until 1991, when the Soviet Union came to its demise. These six periods of our timeline were the following:

1. The End of theWorld War II and Post-War Activities
2. Containment and the Truman Doctrine
3. Crisis and Escalation
4. From Confrontation to Détente
5. The New Cold War
6. The Final Years

In each of these six periods, we discussed the major events that occurred during that time, culminating with the end of the Cold War with the collapse of the Soviet Union in late December 1991.

Our second goal in this section was entered on a discussion of what we see as the five principal causes of the collapse of the Soviet Union. These five reasons we have enumerated and discussed were the following:

1. The Phenomena of Perestroika and Glasnost
2. An Aging Politburo
3. Aggression and Tensions from the West
4. What we have called Guns and Butter
5. The many nationalist movements and Revolutions in the Sixteen Soviet Republics

Next, we have shown how each of these factors or causes greatly contributed to the fall of the Soviet Union, both politically and economically, as well as the dismantling of many of the Soviet social structures. We also indicated that many of these causes and factors were related to Mr. Gorbachev's "Openness" and the desire to eliminate any trace of Stalin-era repression.

In the third goal of Part Four, we concentrated our attention on what we labeled the "Final Days of the Soviet Union," a time that went from March 1991 until Christmas Day of the same year when President Gorbachev of the Soviet Union resigned and the government was taken over by Boris Yeltsin. This period, as we have indicated, also saw the lowering of the Soviet flag at the Kremlin in Moscow for the final time. This event occurred after Gorbachev's ten-minute resignation speech in which he announced the dissolution of the Soviet Union as the eighth and final leader of the Soviet state.

Most of the facts of this ten-month period are not in dispute, but it was a time when most of the fifteen republics of the union had resigned, and many of the political systems among the Soviets had been altered or completely abandoned, such as the KGB, or secret police of the Soviet Union, as well as the government control of newspapers, radio and television.

Finally, we indicated that the "sickness and incapacity" of Mr. Gorbachev at his vacation villa in Crimea had a staged and orchestrated character to it. Even parts of his Christmas resignation speech appeared to have been written by someone else. Thus, in a real way, Boris Yeltsin and his crew appear to have had the final word on the sixty-nine-year-old Soviet Union.

Conclusions to Part Five

In Part Five of this essay on Russian-Ukraine relations dedicated to the Vladimir Putin era, we had four distinctive goals. In the first of those, we spoke about the life of Vladimir Putin, his early life in St. Petersburg, as well as his education and subsequent career in various educational, military and political positions.

Our second goal in Part Five was to explore the main causes of President Putin's intervention in Ukraine. Why does the Russian president want to conquer his neighbor, Ukraine?

To answer that question, we have put forth three reasons. We have labeled these:

1. For historical reasons.
2. For reasons related to the NATO alliance.
3. Mr. Putin's passion for a new Russian empire.

We have explicated and discussed each of these three reasons or factors as they relate to the current war in Ukraine. The first concerns Putin's passion that "Russia and Ukraine are a single people" with the same "moral foundations."

The second reason for the Russian invasion of Ukraine is Mr. Putin's passion for keeping Ukraine from joining NATO, as many former Soviet Republics have already done so. The Russian president called those actions "a tragedy."

Another aspect of Mr. Putin and the NATO alliance is that he realizes the charter of the alliance says, "An incursion in one part of a NATO nation is also an incursion of all of the alliance."

The third goal of Part Five was to ask the question, "Is there a way out of the war in Ukraine?" We, and other experts, have mostly taken a pessimistic view of the war ending anytime in the foreseeable future.

Regarding the question above, we have also enumerated a five-point plan, or "offer of neutrality," suggested by Kiev. But we also pointed out that these five points are heavy concerning Ukraine's defenses and much lighter on the possibility of negotiating a settlement where some lands of Ukraine would be ceded to Russia in exchange for a peace treaty. Say, for example, the Donbas Region.

In the fourth, goal we raised the question of whether President Putin has designs on territories that go beyond the land of Ukraine. In other words, is Putin looking to establish a new Russian empire?

We also pointed out that if the answer to this question is yes, then the next territory in the designs of Vladimir Putin is that of Moldova, like Ukraine is a non-NATO member, as well as being one of the poorest nations in all of Europe. We pointed out that some comments from Rustam Minnekaev, the acting commander of Russia's Central Military District, would appear to support the view that Russia has some designs on Moldova, particularly the

Trans-Dniester Region, a small piece of land between Ukraine ad Moldova.

Finally, we made two other important observations about Russia's interests in Ukraine and perhaps with other former Soviet Republics. The first point is that Russia has shown a pattern of invading territories it desires to acquire, beginning with Crimea in 2014–2015.

This pattern has three steps that look something like this:

First, Russia has shown a desire to acquire some foreign territory.

Second, the establishment or support of separatist groups that are pro-Russian.

And finally, a staged sham election by which Russia's proxy is put securely in power.

The other observation we could add to this analysis is that the pattern mentioned above was not invented by President Putin. Rather, he learned these steps from a master, Josef Stalin, who employed the same techniques when in the process of acquiring lands for the Soviet Union in the 1930s to 1950s.

This same three-step pattern could be seen in the acquisitions of many of the Soviet republics, particularly in the Caucasus and Central Asia in the 1930s. In fact, in non-Russian republics, Russians and Ukrainians were normally second secretaries of Communist parties there and occupied important places in government.

Of course, this was nothing more than the third step of our pattern. Russians were now in power to rule non-Russians in the Soviet Union. Stalin also rearranged political maps. The boundaries of many autonomous republics were fashioned in such a way as to prevent non-Russians in higher offices.

Two fine examples of Stalin's use of his three-step plan were the Tartars and the Bashkirs, two autonomous republics—Tatarstan and Bashkir—though they essentially spoke the same language. The Tartars also occupied regions south of Bashkir and in North Kazakhstan, but the Russian government did not acknowledge all of these clans to be the same people.

What did Stalin do instead? He created separatist groups among the Tartars and Bashkirs. These rebels started insurrections. And they were followed by national elections in which Russians and Ukrainians were put into power.

This, of course, brings us back to Vladimir Putin and whether he has designs to go beyond Ukraine and Moldova. He has already employed Stalin's three-step plan for acquiring territory for Russia in Crimea. He also clearly wishes to reestablish Russia's place on the world stage, and there would be no better place or political design than to create an entirely new Russian empire.

We can bring this point about a new Russian empire to a close when we realize one other pertinent and extremely important point. It is a simple one that can be put very clearly—the Moldovans are certain that they are next.

In an early interview in his presidency, Vladimir Putin was asked who were the men that he most admired? His answer should come as no surprise: Prince Vladimir of Kievan Rus' and Josef Stalin.

There is an old Russian proverb that is sometimes attributed to Prince Vladimir, "Only God can make an elephant out of a fly." Maybe Josef Stalin, and now Vladimir Putin, have put the lie to that proverb. Only time will tell.

Conclusions to Part Six

We have divided Section VI of this study into three parts. In the first of these, we outlined the traditional Marxist-Leninist view that "Religion is the opiate of the masses," a psychological crutch used by the ruling class to subjugate the working class. For Marx and Lenin, religious faith did not serve any purpose in their dialectical materialist view of history, so it was suppressed in both Russia and the Soviet Union.

In the second portion of Section VI, we described the three major faiths in Russia and Ukraine since the Russian Revolution and the eventual establishment of the Soviet Union. These three faiths are the Russian Orthodox Church, the Ukrainian Orthodox Church, and the Catholic Church in Ukraine, mostly in the southwest region of the country. These are the Greek Catholic Church, the Byzantine Rite Ukrainian Greek Catholic Church, and the Ruthenian Latin Rite Church.

One important point we made is that the Catholics, who primarily reside in the southwest of Ukraine, have been subject to religious discrimination since the forming of the Soviet Union.

Finally, in the third portion of Section VI of this study, we made some observations about the role of religion for President Putin and his greatest theological cheerleader, the patriarch of the Russian Orthodox Church, Bishop Kirill.

As we have shown, both men have suggested that the war in Ukraine may best be understood in "metaphysical" rather than material or moral ways. Indeed, both men have referred to the conflict as a new "Holy War" that essentially pits the Russian-influenced world against the West that both Putin and Kirill see as far too secular and too influenced by what the patriarch called "gay parades."

This brings us to the Postscript, appendices, and major sources, followed by the notes of this essay.

A map of the Russian invasion of Ukraine in 2022.

Postscript

Think, when a man or a prince is tough and strong within,
then he can make peace as he pleases; and when he is power-
less, a stronger one will come upon him and do whatever he
wants with him.
—Vlad the Impaler (1428–1476)

There is no such thing as a former KGB agent.
—Vladamir Putin

We write this Postscript on August 22, 2022, the beginning of the twenty-fifth week of the Russian war in Ukraine. On this same day, the United States government announced that it had approved a $775 million military aid package to the nation of Ukraine. In 2022, Ukraine lost 45.1 percent of its gross domestic product, while the other party in the war, Russia, only had a GDP decrease of 9.71 percent.[176]

Since February 2022, 311 companies worldwide have completely withdrawn from Russia, while Ukraine has received financial support from the United States ($125 billion), the European Union ($20 billion), the United Kingdom ($70 billion), Canada ($.3 billion), Germany ($3 billion), Poland ($3 billion), Norway ($1.3 billion), France ($1.2 billion), Japan ($.6 billion), the Netherlands ($.5 billion), Italy ($.5 billion), Czech Republic ($.5 billion), and Sweden ($.5 billion).[177]

Recently, *BBC News* reporter Will Vernon wrote an article entitled, "Ukraine war: Russia appeals for new recruits for war effort." From the city of Volosovo, Mr. Vernon began his article by describing a loudspeaker booming from a pole on the town's main street.[178]

The voice from the speaker announced the formation of two new volunteer artillery battalions for men aged eighteen to sixty. The same announcement can also be heard on social media, Russian television, and billboards throughout the Russian Federation.

Since the start of the war, some recent reports estimated that 70,000 to 80,000 Russian soldiers had lost their lives. Mr. Vernon reported that the announcement from the loudspeaker indicated that the recruits, through their families, would be paid 47,000 Euros a month, approximately $57,000 in American currency. However, returning Russian recruits from the war stated that they, and their families, received none of the money promised.

Other economic estimates in late August 2022 provide another window into why President Vladimir Putin of Russia is so worried about Ukraine not becoming a member of NATO. Research expert M. Shahbandeh reports that in terms of military personnel, NATO has 5.4 million soldiers, while Russia has only 1.4 million. NATO has 3.4 million active soldiers, while Russia has only 850,000. NATO has 1.4 million reserve troops, to 250,000 Russian reserves. NATO personnel includes 750,000 paramilitary soldiers, while the Russian Federation has only 250,000.[179]

A similar disparity can be seen in terms of the phenomenon of air power between NATO and Russia. Three examples will suffice to indicate the disparity. NATO has 25,000 aircraft to Russia's 4,200. Secondly, NATO possesses 678 tanker aircraft, while the Russian Federation has only twenty. Lastly, NATO has 8,500 helicopters in its arsenal, and Russia has only 1,500.[180]

Before the war in Ukraine began, Russia had 17,000 tanks. By July 15, 2022, it only had 2,800 left. Similar figures can also be seen in the number of aircraft lost since the beginning of the hostilities. Indeed, to date, the Ukrainian forces have destroyed forty-seven aircraft, without a corresponding number of Ukrainian planes taken out of service.[181]

It may well be the case that another reason why Mr. Putin is concerned that Ukraine remains neutral in relation to Russia and the West is that he knows full well that if Ukraine joins NATO, his army will be outmanned and would have a vastly inferior armament vis-à-vis NATO.[182]

Dr. Shahbandeh also reports that since late February 2022, the nation of Ukraine had next to zero border crossings, but by August 11, 2022, that number had reached over ten million. Similarly, there were no significant border crossings into Ukraine on February 24, 2022, but border crossings into Ukraine by August 11, 2022, totaled over four million.[183]

Another significant group of figures relates to the public opinion regarding the war in Ukraine. A representative sample of the population of Ukraine shows that "If a referendum was proposed to include Ukraine into NATO, would you support this measure?" Sixty percent of Ukrainians said yes, while 28 percent said no, with 15 percent either refused to answer or thought it was too difficult to answer.[184]

Another significant disparity between Russia and Ukraine in the six months of the war is the number of civilians injured and killed. Russia does not publish any figures about its civilian injuries or deaths, while Ukraine reported in July 2022 that 7,698 civilians were injured and 595 died during the war.[185] Some early estimates in the early weeks of the war in Ukraine suggested that the Russian Army lost 100 to 200 soldiers a day.[186] That figure now, however, appears to be much higher.

And so, the war in Ukraine wages on. The BBC has assembled a series of maps it calls the "Ukraine War in Maps." Among these maps are headings such as "Clashes in the South," "Russia in Eastern Ukraine," "Russia in the Donbas Region," and finally, "Areas of Russian Control." The latter of these offers a depiction of how little area of Ukraine the Russian Army at this point has control over.[187]

Early in the war, when Russia attempted to gain control of Kiev, the Russian Army was dismally unsuccessful. The Ukrainian people rallied themselves against Mr. Putin and his regime and failed to achieve success in Ukraine's capital. Ironically, this is precisely the place where this essay began, with Prince Vladimir the First and the beginning of the Kingdom of Kievan Rus'.

Three final points will end this Postscript and essay *From Vladimir to Vladimir*. First, the current Russo-Ukrainian War has been in progress since February of 2014, following what has been called the Ukrainian "Revolution of Dignity."[188] At that time, pro-Russian separatists focused on the regions of Crimea and the Donbas, both of which have been internationally recognized as parts of Ukraine.

The first eight years of the conflict included the Russian annexation of Crimea in 2014 and the war in the Donbas from 2014 to the present time. The Russian government began a military buildup on its border with Ukraine in November and December of 2021. The conflict only considerably expanded when Russia launched a full-scale invasion starting on February 24, 2022.

Secondly, when pro-Russian President Viktor Yanukovych of Ukraine was removed from office, Pro-Russian unrest erupted in parts of the country. Russian soldiers without insignia took control of the infrastructure of the country, as well as taking control of the Crimean Parliament.[189]

Finally, and perhaps most importantly, when Russia took control of Crimea, it employed the age-old Stalinist technique of identifying a territory for occupation, followed by inserting separatists into the conflict and then calling for an election in which Russia takes control of the president and the Parliament.

In August 2014, unmarked Russian military vehicles crossed the border with Ukraine into the Donetsk republic. An undeclared war began between Ukrainian forces on the one side and Russian soldiers and separatists on the other. This conflict soon settled into a static state with repeated failed attempts at a ceasefire.

In 2015, the Minsk II agreement was signed by Russia and Ukraine, but ongoing fighting prevented this agreement from being implemented. By 2019, Ukraine officially stated that seven percent of their country was now "temporary, occupied territory."[190]

Given what we have seen in the BBC's "Ukraine War in Maps," 7 percent is now much higher. As we have suggested earlier in this essay, one only wonders what President Putin has in his plan after the Russo-Ukrainian War is over.

When Putin ordered his troops to invade Ukraine on February 24, 2022, he believed that his army would crush the Ukrainian defenses, followed by a very swift victory in the war. Remarkably, however, that did not occur. Most of the pundits and the early expert opinions on the war predicted that the war would fall to Russia's control in a matter of months, if not weeks or days. It was a bleak and pessimistic picture, but such forecasting could not have been more wrong.

Early Russian missteps, such as the MIA Russian air force and the lack of combined arms operations, created a number of early opportunities for the Ukrainian defenses. Serious supply issues and disorders, as well as discipline problems in the ranks, hindered the early efforts of the Russian Army.

When Putin's troops initially encircled Kiev, the forces failed to gain control of the city. Thus, they were unable to topple the Ukrainian government, as they had done in 2014 on the Crimean Peninsula. Unable to seize Kiev, Russia pulled back and redirected its focus to concentrate in the Donbas Region in the east, where conflicts had gone on for eight years. Now—six months into the War—Russia's rapid advance has slowed to a crawl, while the Ukrainian forces are making sure that the Russians pay in blood for every small bit of land in Ukraine.

One thing that Mr. Putin clearly did not envision before the Russian attack that began on February 24, 2022, was the bravery, the tenacity, and the valor of the Ukrainian soldiers as well as the Ukrainian citizens. Those phenomena have indeed been a miracle to behold.

How long the conflict in Ukraine will last is anyone's best guess, but military history has much to show us about what happens when great military powers begin to falter as Russia has done in its war with its neighbor to the south.

Russian forces could suffer a catastrophic defeat akin to that of Egyptian President Gamal Abdul Nasser's army in the 1967 so-called "Six-Day War," when more than eighty percent of Egyptian forces and equipment were lost.[191] Is such a defeat possible for Vladimir Putin and his generals, many of whom have become part of the Russian carnage in the war?

Last summer, the Afghan security forces and government collapsed amid weak governance and widespread corruption. So have many other large and well-equipped armies in the last century—the demoralized Russian Army in 1917, the out-maneuvered French forces in 1940 at the beginning of World War II, and the British Army's fate in Singapore in 1942. Not to mention the defeats of the South Vietnamese Army in 1975 and the Iraqi forces in Mosul in 2014.

In all of these examples from modern military history, there could be seen a lack of cohesion and organization in military institutions and structures. These are also examples of an old canard that Carl von Clausewitz emphasized many years ago—military victory is not possible without the cooperation of the army, the government, and the people at large.[192]

In an April 2022 article for *The Hill*, Peter A. Wilson of the RAND Corporation pointed to three implications if the Russian Army is defeated in Ukraine. These can be summarized this way:

- First, it might encourage Western nations to boost, train, and equip other countries near Russia.
- Second, a Russian Army collapse might force Western intelligence analysts to reevaluate the vulnerability of the Baltic countries, as well as others in Eastern Europe in terms of Russian aggression.
- Third, we may see, as a consequence of a Russian military defeat in Ukraine, a great military increase or proliferation of weapons.[193]

All of these implications, of course, will have little value if we remember that unlike President Nasser in Egypt, Vladimir Putin has an arsenal of nuclear weapons that he often mentions and has threatened to employ. But this has not deterred the Ukrainians.

The role of nuclear power has also arisen in another context of the Ukraine War. In March 2022, shortly after the beginning of the war, Russian troops seized the Ukraine nuclear power plant at Zaporizhzhia. It soon began to be managed by the Russian nuclear power company, Rosatom, while the Ukrainian scientists who worked there continued to do most of the work, though now under Russian control.

By July 2022, Russian forces deployed rocket launchers into the complex and, in effect, turned the power plant into a military base. On August 3, 2022, the International Atomic Energy Agency reported that the plant "is completely out of control" and needed inspection and repairs.[194] Two days later, on August 5, Ukraine's nuclear agency Energoatom reported that two rounds of Russian rocket strikes near the plant prompted its operators to disconnect one of its reactors from the main power grid.[195]

Three days after that, on August 8, 2022, Ukraine reported that Russia had renewed the shelling of Zaporizhzhia and damaged three radiation sensors while injuring one worker. Local Russian officials in Ukraine said the site was hit by multiple rocket launches.[196] On August 10, foreign ministers from the G7 nations observed that Russia must immediately hand back control of the plant to the Ukrainians.[197] Then, on August 11, there was more shelling of the nuclear plant in Ukraine, but this time both Russia and Ukraine blamed the action on each other.[198]

Most recently, on August 26, after two of its six nuclear reactors were reconnected to the grid following more shelling that caused Europe's largest nuclear power plant—the one at Zaporizhzhia— President Zelensky ordered them to be disconnected in its history for the first time, remarked during his daily briefing, "Let me stress that the situation remains very risky and dangerous."[199]

Residents near the power plant reportedly were given iodine tablets amid mounting fears that the fighting around the complex could trigger some kind of nuclear catastrophe. Meanwhile, the *Wall Street Journal* reported that "It is almost certain that a mission from the International Atomic Energy Agency will visit the plant in the final week of August 2022, although details are still being completed."[200]

There is no doubt that all of this activity from March to late August 2022 came at the hands and orders of Russian President Vladimir Putin, yet another instance in which he could threaten Ukraine and the rest of the world with the possibility of a nuclear war.

Thus, we will end this study of the history of the relations of Russia to Ukraine with a bold prediction about how the war in Ukraine will finally come to an end. It will happen—as modern military history suggests—with the final collapse of the Russian Army and the victory of Ukraine and its dedicated people.

Meanwhile, there are signs that the Russian Army and the Putin administration are in trouble at the end of August 2022. One report shows that the GDP in Russia has shrunk by 10 percent in 2022, while Germany, France, China, and the US have all decreased between 4 and 6 percent. The only positive GDP in the study is Saudi Arabia, whose economy grew 8 percent in 2022.[201]

Ukrainian troops have "broken" the first line of Russian defense in Kherson. International inspectors are "on their way" to the

Zaporizhzhia nuclear power plant, while fears the war could induce a radioactive disaster are on the rise. And President Vladimir Putin's Defense Minister, Sergei Shoigu, has been "sidelined."[202] None of these are good signs. The end may certainly be near.

Vladimir Putin (right) with his long-time confidant
Defense Minister Sergey Shoigu, 2017.

Appendix I
When Will the War in Ukraine End?

This is a Nuremberg moment in terms of just the sheer scale
of the breach of rule-based international order that has been
perpetrated by Russia in this invasion.

—Ambassador Beth Van Schaack

The International Criminal Court has been examining evidence of war crimes in Ukraine since Russia's invasion of the
Crimea in 2014.

—James A. Goldston, "How to Hold Russia
accountable for War Crimes in Ukraine"

Introduction

We have the following aims in this appendix. First, to make some
observations about the outcomes or results of the war in Ukraine since
February 24, 2022. The second goal or aim is to sketch out the possible
outcomes of the war in Ukraine for the future. What are the possible
"avenues" about when the war will end?

In the third section, we will make some final observations about
Russia's incursion into the sovereign state of Ukraine. Will Russia, for
example, be charged with war crimes, as well as other questions about
the war? This section of the appendix is called "Final Thoughts."

Outcomes and Results So Far of the War in Ukraine

Since the beginning of the war in Ukraine, nearly two-thirds of the children are either displaced in their own country or have become refugees in various other places in Europe, particularly Poland.[203] Millions of lives, in other words, have been turned inside out, while a return to normalcy in Ukraine now seems far beyond reach.

As yet, there are no reliable figures of how many non-combatants have been killed in Ukraine by Russian bullets, bombs, missiles and artillery shells. And all of this has been made much worse by what many in the West have called "war crimes," including President Joe Biden.

So, how is it possible that this traumatized nation of Ukraine will ever become whole again, and in such a disastrous situation, what could the future possibly hold for President Zelensky and his nation?

It is easy to forget how daring and rash President Vladimir Putin's decision to invade Ukraine was. After all, next to Russia, Ukraine is Europe's largest country in land area and is the sixth biggest in population. It is true that Mr. Putin acted aggressively when he annexed the Crimea Peninsula in 2014 and 2015.

Putin also fostered and sponsored the rise of two breakaway enclaves in parts of the Donbas Region in the eastern Ukrainian provinces of Lugansk and Donetsk that are also industrial centers and locales that are rich in resources in areas that adjoin Russia.[204] Nor was President Putin's 2015 intervention in the Syrian civil war in order to save the government of Bashar al-Assad, that many in the West, and the Middle East, believed was a wide-eyed gamble.

Mr. Putin made Russia's participation in the Syrian war related to airstrikes and missile attacks while not using ground forces.[205] In the back of his mind, the Russian president must have been thinking—and remembering—the kind of quagmire that could have resulted like Russia's war in Afghanistan.[206]

The incursion of Ukraine appears to have been a genuinely rash act. Russia began the war with what seemed like a massive military advantage, as well as a gross domestic product (GDP), to the numbers of warplanes, tanks, artillery, warships and missiles. There was little wonder that on February 24, 2022, Mr. Putin believed that the war would end in weeks, at the very most.[207] He was particularly hopeful at the time that his army would have captured Kiev in those few weeks and completely underestimated the tenacity and heart of the Ukrainian people.

Mr. Putin was not alone in his prediction of how long the war in Ukraine would last. Many Western military experts, including many in America, were convinced the war would end sometime in April 2022. They thought Russia's army would make quick work of its Ukrainian counterpart, even if the latter's army had mostly been trained by the United States, Britain and Canada since 2015.

In those first few weeks of the war, the morale of Ukraine's citizens and army remained quite high, and the Ukrainian commanders' strategies were working adeptly. By the end of March, Russia had already lost tanks and aircraft valued at five billion dollars, not to mention the fact that Russia had sent a full 25 percent of its troops into battle.[208]

Russia's military supply abilities proved surprisingly inept, whether it was parts for repairing equipment or the simple delivery of food, water and medical supplies to the troops at the front.

By May and June, Russian forces made significant gains in the south and southeast, occupying part of the Black Sea coast of the Kherson Province, which is just north of the Crimea Peninsula.[209] They also captured most of the Donbas Province in the east, beginning in May, and in the southeast, Zaporizhzhia. The Russian troops also created a patchy land corridor connecting Russia to Crimea since it was taken in 2014 and 2015.

Still, the Russians botched its assault in the north and its attempt to capture Kiev, spending vast sums of money. Meanwhile, in the United States and elsewhere in the West, the intrepid Ukrainian resistance and its successes on the battlefield have produced a narrative that the war is a David and Goliath story, with Ukraine as David, and Russia and Mr. Putin, of course, as Goliath.[210]

By late May, however, things began to change. Bit by bit, Russia's advantage, with shorter supply zones and better terrain suited for tanks and military trucks, as well as their overwhelming advantage in armaments—particularly artillery—began to pay off. Perhaps most ominously, Russian troops encircled a large portion of Ukraine's most battle-tested soldiers in Donbas, where towns like Lyman and Popasna made the headlines for atrocities there.

So, what to make of all of this? In the next section of this appendix, we will sketch out three possible scenarios for what may come next so that this most devastating war might come to an end. We also will suggest four Ukraine scenarios that most likely will not bring the war to a close.

Four Scenarios for the End of War in Ukraine

We can quickly dismiss one of the four scenarios because it seems most likely not to occur. This is President Zelensky's idea of ending the war. That is, Russia withdrew, and all the areas taken in the war since February 24, 2022, be returned to the nation of Ukraine. Given Mr. Putin's track record in the past, this scenario seems highly unlikely to come to pass.

The other three much more viable possibilities for ending the war in Ukraine we shall call:

1. The De Facto Partition View
2. The Neutrality with Sweeteners Approach
3. The New Russian Empire Solution[211]

In this section, we will describe and discuss these three possibilities for bringing Russia's incursion into the sovereign state of Ukraine to some resolution without arguing for any preference of the three.

De Facto Partition

If it is the case that Russia's army takes all of the Donbas Region plus the whole of the Black Sea coast, it would make Ukraine considerably smaller, as well as being landlocked. If that were to occur, this might prompt Mr. Putin to declare a victory in what he has labeled his "special military operation."[212] Mr. Putin would declare a ceasefire, order his commanders to fortify and secure the new areas of occupation, and saddle the Ukrainians with the challenge of expelling the Russian troops or settling for this de facto partition possibility.

In this scenario, Mr. Putin could respond with new air attacks and missile strikes, which would only exacerbate the great economic hit Ukraine already has taken. Some estimates now say that destroyed and damaged infrastructure and industry in the country have added five billion dollars to the Ukraine budget. The estimated decrease in the GNP is predicted to be around 45 percent this year alone.[213] But clearly, billions of dollars in revenues have been lost to Ukraine because it cannot ship its main exports by way of the Russia-dominated Black Sea.

One April estimate on the cost of rebuilding Ukraine's infrastructure and economy ranges from five hundred billion dollars to one trillion dollars, a price tag far beyond the means of a new government in Kiev.[214]

If Kiev did, however, accept the idea of a partition, it would forfeit substantial territory, and it is likely that President Zelensky would face considerable backlash at home. Still, in this scenario, he may have little choice as his nation could see an economic and military strain of an endless war that would be unbearable.

Meanwhile, Western Allies to Ukraine may become "war-weary." They are just beginning to feel an economic effect that some economists say might be as much as 2 percent in 2023 and 2024. And all of this as mid-term election loom in the United States, as President Biden's approval ratings continue to sink.

Meanwhile, the inflation rate in Europe was 8.1 percent in May, the highest it has been since 1996. Energy prices have exploded there. Within days of the invasion of Ukraine, European natural gas prices rose seventy percent, while oil hit $105 a barrel, an eight-year high. Inflation in Britain in May was also at 8.2 percent. On June 8, 2022, gasoline prices in the United Kingdom reached a seventeen-year high.[215]

The Organisation for Economic Co-operation and Development (OECD) recently predicted that the economies of France, Germany and Italy—the three largest in Europe—will all contract for the remainder of 2022. Only France has reported an anemic growth of 0.2 percent in the fourth quarter. Meanwhile, the Biden Administration has begun to re-define what a "recession" is, arguing that two-quarters of no economic growth—the traditional definition—no longer applies in America.[216]

Of course, all of these economic troubles may produce a kind of Ukraine fatigue in the West. The possibility of negotiation with Mr. Putin has been raised by France, Italy and Germany with no success; even a visit from the German chancellor to visit with Putin brought no substantial results.

Western support, in time, may be seen as progressively weaker. All of this, in turn, could set the stage for a de facto partition scenario in Ukraine. Certainly, a very distinct possibility for the future.

Neutrality with Sweeteners

Another possibility for ending the war in Ukraine is the Neutrality with Sweeteners Approach. Before the war, Mr. Putin pushed for a neutral Ukraine that would forbid any military alliances for the nation. Both NATO and Mr. Zelensky said no. NATO's 2008 Bucharest summit that both Ukraine and Georgia brought great consternation to President Putin and made the idea of neutrality all the more central for the Russian leader.[217]

In late March, a month after the war in Ukraine began, president Zelensky put the idea of neutrality on the table, but by then, it was too late. President Putin already had put his aims on the battlefield to be central.

If the conflict continues much longer, it might revive the neutrality approach, particularly if Ukraine was promised concessions for remaining in a neutral posture, what we have called "Sweeteners" here.

Mr. Putin would also like to do something about the many sanctions set by Western nations regarding the Russian government. Add to this Russia's now apparent dependence on China, so Russia has to find a way of easing Western sanctions while, in the meantime, being dependent on the People's Republic of China.

These circumstances might revive the neutrality option. Russia would return its land corridor to Crimea, even if some concessions to Ukraine are made. One of those might be that the water canals flowing southward to the peninsula from the city of Kherson that would revert to Ukrainian control would never again be blocked.

In this scenario, Russia would not annex the "republics" it created in Stalin's day. And most importantly, in time, Ukraine would be given the fast track to NATO membership, as well as long-term economic aid for reconstruction and the rebuilding of the nation. But an aid package from America and Europe would be costly, so they would have to decide how much they would offer to end the most destructive military conflict in Europe since the end of World War II in 1945.

The New Russian Empire Solution

Since the war began in Ukraine, many commentators and Western leaders, including President Biden, called for a regime change in Russia and Mr. Putin's departure.[218] Indeed, many prognosticators have predicted that the invasion will prove to be the Russian president's death knell.

At this point, however, there is no evidence that his war has turned the country's political and military elite against him. In other words, there are no signs of a coup, the method by which many Socialist governments have come to an end in the last seventy years. It is unlikely, of course, that Mr. Putin would go voluntarily. And even if he did, he would most likely be replaced by someone in his inner circle, which constantly continues to be changing, as well.

Another possibility is that Russia becomes a true democracy following prolonged public demonstrations, much like in other Soviet republics in the late 1980s and early 1990s. If this were to happen, we would hope that it would be peacefully accomplished, for Russia has approximately six thousand nuclear warheads, shares land borders with fourteen other states, and maritime borders with three more countries.[219] Russia is also the world's largest country with more than seventeen million kilometers, 44 percent larger than the runner up, Canada. So, if we are hoping for a democratic change in Russia, we better hope that that transformation happens peacefully. Upheaval in a vast nuclear-armed country would be a disaster.

But there is also one final scenario, and this is one we discussed at the close of Part Five of this essay on Russia-Ukraine relations. And that possibility is this: After Ukraine, Mr. Putin has designs on Moldova, then Belarus and, perhaps, beyond. As we have shown, some of the leaders in Moldova are convinced that this is what is really on the mind of President Vladimir Putin.[220]

We also pointed out the consternation that Mr. Putin has expressed about the collapse of the Soviet Union and the demise of a Russian empire. It may indeed be the case that the invasion of Ukraine is merely the first step in establishing the "New Russian Empire," an empire that would depend on two things.

First, the new territory of the new empire will come from the former republics of the Soviet Union. And second, the acquiring of that land will come by way of Josef Stalin's three-prong approach to acquiring new territory. That is, first, the desire to acquire. Second, the backing of insurrectionists. And finally, a new pro-Russia-backed election ending in the establishment of a proxy as head of the government.

Further evidence that the war in Ukraine will end with the collapse of the Russian Army can be seen in a *New York Times* article written by reporter Anton Troianovski, entitled, "Russia's Retreat in Ukraine Pokes Holes in Putin's Projection."[221] In the report, Mr. Troianovski suggested that the war may be entering a new phase after Ukraine forces dealt a large blow to Russia's grip on parts of Eastern Ukraine that Russia had occupied for months.[222]

Russian forces, for example, had to flee the strategic eastern city of Izium after it had been occupied for five months. Russian forces had to flee just five days after Ukraine troops began a new offensive eastward through the region of Kharkiv. A spokesman for the Bohun Brigade of the Ukrainian land forces said in a statement on September 10, 2022, "The Russians escaped and left their weapons and ammo behind."[223]

The following day—the twenty-first anniversary of 9/11—spokesmen for the Ukrainian Army indicated that Russian troops had abandoned the town of Svatove in the Luhansk region, a town that, until Saturday, was still forty kilometers, or twenty-five miles, beyond the known front line of the Ukraine advance. Svatove had been an important hub in Russian supply routes that now will be permanently interrupted.

In the region of Kharkiv, more than forty settlements had been liberated from Russian control. One administrator of the region told Ukrainian television, "We can officially announce the liberation of more than forty settlements. The situation is changing incredibly quickly and there are many, many more such de-occupied settlements."[224] In fact, in many of these settlements, the Ukrainian flag has begun to be flown.

Commander and Chief of Ukraine's forces, General Valery Zaluzhnyi, remarked that since the beginning of September more than "three thousand square kilometers have been returned to the control of its rightful owner, Ukraine."[225] The he added, "Ukrainian forces have begun to advance not only to the south and east in the Kharkiv Region but also to the north. There are fifty kilometers to go to the state border."[226]

CNN reported that the Ukrainian flag was raised in settlements very close to the Russian border, confirming the continuing retreat of Russian forces in the area. Olek Kulik, an official in the town of Derhachi, northeast of the city of Kharkiv, suggested the flag of Ukraine had been raised there by local residents. The same is true in the town of Kozacha Lopan, which the Russians have occupied since March. The town is only five kilometers from the Russian border and has extensively been damaged in the conflict.[227]

Another Ukrainian town named Tokarivka has also begun to raise the Ukrainian flag daily. Tokarivka is only a few kilometers from the Russian border. One official in the town described the situation as "The Ukrainians came, and the residents heard the 'roar of Russian military hardware leaving.' They left a lot of ammunition behind."[228]

When the forces of Ukraine entered the city of Izium on Saturday, September 10, it was more than a military victory. It was a sign that the war in Ukraine might be entering a new phase, one in which Russian forces are scrambling to hold onto territory previously captured over the past six months.

As indicated earlier, there are many possible ways that the war in Ukraine may eventually come to an end. And one of the most important of those ways may, in fact, be with the eventual collapse of the Russian Army.

On September 11, in his daily news conference, President Volodymyr Zelensky spoke of one alleged episode in which he said, "One hundred and fifty service members of the armed forces of the Russian Federation left in a convoy from Borshchova and Artemivka in the Kharkiv Region. If this report is true, then it is further evidence that we may be beginning to see the eventual collapse of the Russian Army, while at home, President Putin's war is becoming increasingly less popular."[229]

A recent report from NPR from early September 2022 suggested that only fifty percent of Russian citizens support Mr. Putin's war in Ukraine. This is down from the sixty percent reported by the same new organization on April 18, 2022, and the eighty percent reported at the beginning of the war in late February of the same year.[230]

This brings us to some final thoughts in this appendix of this essay on Russian-Ukrainian relations, from the time of one Vladimir to the contemporary time of another Vladimir, the current Russian president.

Final Thoughts

The amount of destruction and loss of life should be enough compelling reasons to end the war in Ukraine. It also continues to create unforeseen misery and hardship in some of the world's poorest nations, such as Kenya, Ethiopia, Yemen and Somalia. Along with devastating droughts and local conflicts, the war has led to staggering increases in foot prices connected to Russian and Ukrainian grains.

More than twenty-seven million people worldwide now face acute food shortages or even outright starvation in the four nations we have mentioned above alone, thanks at least in part to the war in Ukraine.

The current war in Europe is the largest in seventy-five years, but it is not Europe's war alone. The pain it produces extends to people in faraway lands already barely surviving and with no way to end the suffering.

It is rarely the case that analysts of an event like the war in Ukraine ever consider the cost to others that go beyond the immediate environment of the trouble and conflict at hand. There may be many political and economic woes that are not directly associated with an event such as the war in Ukraine.

Secondly, it appears unlikely that Ukraine will continue to fight with sustained Western support and eventually forces Russia to withdraw its troops from Ukraine entirely, with the possible exception of Crimea and the Donbas Region.

Thirdly, if what we have labeled the "New Russian Empire" scenario were to come to fruition in Eastern Europe, Russia would proceed with Stalin's three-prong plan, followed by a new "Russification" of the territories claim so they may more easily be incorporated into the New Russian Empire.

Finally, the question of whether Russia has committed war crimes in the eyes of the international community certainly should be on the table. Mr. Biden has already expressed his opinion that war crimes have been committed.

War crimes and what are called "crimes against humanity" are international crimes of such a magnitude that they shock the conscience of all of humanity. Examples of war crimes include acts of violence, attacks, and reprisals against civilians, as well as civilian infrastructure.[231] Thus, many of the burned-out public buildings we have seen in Ukraine meet the standard for a war crime.

Top Biden Administration officials are working behind the scenes with the government of Ukraine and American European allies to document a tsunami of war crimes allegedly committed by Russian forces.

The sheer volume of documented war crime cases, however, is too overwhelming for Ukraine's justice system, as well as for the International Criminal Court, or ICC. Questions need to be raised on how many cases should be brought to trial and how many accused Russian war criminals could ultimately face justice. And, more importantly, is the Russian soldier or President Putin the real war criminal?[232]

When the war in Ukraine ends, we should see a "Nuremberg moment" related to the war there. Beth Van Schaack, the US Ambassador-at-large for criminal justice, agrees with this sentiment. She recently wrote,

> This is a Nuremberg moment in terms of just the sheer scale of the breach of the rules-based international order that has been perpetrated by Russia in this invasion.

She adds:

> Even the most well-resourced prosecutorial office would have a hard time grappling with the sheer scale of the criminality that has been on display.[233]

We can only end this essay by simply saying, Amen to that!

Appendix II
Foreign Words and Phrases

Akmat	A member of the Khan family (Mongolian)
Ar Rus	Russia (Arabic)
Batu	A member of the Khan family (Mongolian)
blitzkrieg	lightning attack (German)
Bolschistvo	verb origin of Bolshevik (Russian)
Bolshevik	majority (Russian)
czar/czarina	male and female rulers (Russian)
Dazhbog	Slavic god in charge of dishing out wealth and providing rays of the sun (Russian)
détente	The relaxation of strained relations (French)
Dzbog	Slavic god of winds (Russian)
einsatzgruppen	death squad (German)
Esugal	Genghis Khan's father (Mongolian)
glasnost	openness (Russian)
holodomor	death by hunger (Ukrainian)
Hulega Khan	Mongolian leader (Mongolian)

Jochi	A member of the Khan family (Mongolian)
Komitet Gosudarstvennoy Bezopasnosti	KGB, Russian secret police (Russian)
Kremlin	fortress (Russian)
Krovavoye Voskresenye	Bloody Sunday, St. Petersburg riot, 1905 (Russian)
Kublai	A member of the Khan family (Mongolian)
Luftwaffe	air force (German)
Mokosh/Mokosa	Slavic goddess of fate and protector of women in childbirth (Russian)
Mongke	A member of the Khan family (Mongolian)
Moskovskiy Kreml	Moscow Kremlin, the fortified complex in the center of Moscow (Russian)
Nahseh	The day of the setback (Arabic)
oblasti	Subdivision of property (Ukrainian)
Ogodei	A member of the Khan family (Mongolian)
Pereiaslav	Cossack city and name of a 1654 treaty (Russian)
perestroika	restructuring (Russian)
Perun	Slavic god of the sky, thunder and war (Russian)
pravda	truth (Russian)
rasputitsta	muddy quagmire (Russian)
Revoliutsiia hidnosti	Revolution of Dignity (Russian)

Rod	Slavic god, creator of all things that exist, including the other gods (Russian)
Rods	Russia (Old Norse)
Ruotsi	Russia (Finnish)
Rus'	early name for Russia
Ruscia or Ruzzia	Russia (Old German)
Rusia	Russia (Latin)
Russie	Russia (Old French)
Russkaya Pravda	medieval Russian manuscript (Russian)
Russkiy Mir or Russaya Mir	Russian world or Russian Domain (Russian)
Semargl	Slavic god of fire and fertility (Russian)
Smutnoye Vremya	Time of Trouble (Russian)
Spasskaya	One of the towers of the Kremlin complex (Russian)
Temuchin	Mongol name of Genghis Khan (Mongolian)
tzar/tzarina	male and female rulers (Russian)
Veles	Slavic god of the Underworld and the harvests and was the deity that brought cattle and other animals to people (Russian)
Veliky the Great	Pyotr Vekily or Peter the Great (Russian)
Vom Kriege	On War (German)

Appendix III: Summary of Events from the Collapse of the Soviet Union until the War in Ukraine

July 1990	Ukrainian vote on independence.
August 23, 1991	Ukraine declares independence.
November 1991	Leonid Kravchuk elected president of Ukraine.
December 26, 1991	Gorbachev gives Christmas speech.
December 5, 1994	Ukraine signed Budapest memorandum in its nuclear arsenal.
November 1999	Kravchuk re-elected.
November 2004	Pro-Russian candidate, Viktor Yanukovich, is declared president of Ukraine in a rigged election.
2008	NATO promises Ukraine it will soon join NATO.
2010	Russia and Ukraine agree on a gasoline pricing deal.
2013	Yanukovich's government suspends trade with the EU.
February 2014	Yanukovich ousted as president. Russian annexation of Crimea begins.
April 2014	Pro-Russian separatist in the Donbas Region declare independence.

May 2014	Petro Poroshenko wins election for president.
July 2014	Russian missile brings down flight MH17.
2017	Agreement signed between Ukraine and EU on open markets.
2019	New Ukrainian Orthodox Church established angering the Kremlin. Former comic Volodymyr Zelensky elected president.
March 2020	Ukraine declares its first Covid lockdown.
February 24, 2022	President Putin authorizes "Special Military Operation" on war in Ukraine.

Major Sources of this Essay

Introduction

Most of the sources for this essay on Russia-Ukraine relations are contained in the notes of the first five sections of this essay. However, there are also several books and monographs that have been extremely helpful in writing it. They were mostly brought to our attention by our son John "Jack" Vicchio. In some cases, we also made some slight comments about the importance of particular items.

We will also speak of materials from other media with which we have relied, particularly audiobooks and some literary works. Among these books and monographs were the following:

Beevor, Antony. *Stalingrad: The Fateful Siege, 1942–1943*. New York: Penguin Books, 1998.

Buchanan, Sir George. *My Mission to Russia*. London: Hard Press Books, 2012.

Bushkovitch, Paul. *A Concise History of Russia*. Cambridge: Cambridge University Press, 2017.

Carell, Paul. *Hitler's War on Russia*. London: Macmillan, 1964.

Carr, E. H. *The Bolshevik Revolution*. New York: Macmillan and Company, 1950.

Chamberlin, W. H. *The Russian Revolution*. London, 1935. Chamberlin was the Russian correspondent for the *Christian Science Monitor.*

Charques, R. D. *The Twilight of Imperial Russia*. New York: Normanby Press, 2017.

Chernov, V. M. *The Great Russian Revolution.* Moscow, 1917. This is an eyewitness account of the Russian Revolution.

Craig, William. *Enemy at the Gates: The Battle for Stalingrad.* Open Road Media, 2015.

Daniels, R. V. *Red October.* Boston: Beacon Press, 1984.

Fitzpatrick, Sheila. *The Russian Revolution.* Oxford: Oxford University Press, 2017.

Florinsky, M. T. *The End of the Russian Empire.* London: Borodino Books, 2017.

Garrard, C., ed. *World War II and the Soviet People.* New York: Palgrave Macmillan, 1993.

Kerensky, A. M. *Russia and History's Turning Point.*

Miliukov, P. *Russia and Its Crisis.* Chicago: Wentworth Press, 2019.

Moore, B. *History of Soviet Politics.*

Pares, Bernard. *The Fall of the Russian Monarch.* New York: J. Cape, 1939.

Smith, S. A. *Russia in Revolution: An Empire in Crisis, 1890 to 1928.* Oxford: Oxford University Press, 2017.

Stavrou, T. G. *Russia Under the Last Tsar.* Minneapolis: University of Minnesota Press, 1969.

Trotsky, Leon. *The History of the Russian Revolution.* Ann Arbor: University of Michigan Press, 1967.

Troyat, Henri. *Daily Life in Russia under the Last Tsar.* Palo Alto: Stanford University Press, 1979.

Ulam, Adam B. *The Bolsheviks.* London: Macmillan, 1965.

Von Laue, Theodore. *Why Lenin? Why Stalin?* Philadelphia: J. B. Lippincott, 1964.

von Rauch, G. *A History of Soviet Russia.* New York: Frederick A. Praeger, 1957.

Wallace, D. Mackenzie. *Russia on the Eve of War and Revolution.* Vintage Books, 1961.

Weale, Adrian. *Army of Evil: A History of the SS.* New York: Dutton Books, 2010.

Zygar, Mikhail. *All the Kremlin's Men.* Washington: Public Affairs, 2017.

Other Media Sources

In completing this essay on Russian-Ukraine relations, we also relied on materials from other media, such as audiobooks and several Russian novels we have re-read. In fact, no one can capture the flavor and mood of Russia better than its finest novelists.

In that regard, in preparation for the construction of this essay, we have re-read the following volumes:

Alexei Tolstoy. *Road to Calvary*

Mikhail Sholokhov. *Quietly Flows the Don* and *The Don Flows to the Sea*

Boris Pasternak. *Doctor Zhivago*

Among the audiobooks we consulted are the following:

Richard Pipes. *The Russian Revolution*. With Michael page as narrator.

Sean McMeekin. *The Russian Revolution: A New History*. With Pete Larkin as narrator.

An audiobook version of Leon Trotsky's *History of the Russian Revolution*. With Jonathan Booth as narrator.

And an audiobook version of William Craig's *Enemy at the Gates*. Narrated by David Baker.

Endnotes

1   The two best sources for Prince Vladimir are Sergey Solovyov, *Prince St. Vladimir and Yaroslav* (IDDK: 2012); and Vladimir Volkoff, *Vladimir the Russian Viking: The Legendary Prince Who Transformed a Nation* (New York: Overlook Books, 2011).

2   Bai Ying Borjigin, *History of the Family of Genghis Khan* (New York: Taylor and Seale, 2022).

3   The term "Russification" refers to political policies designed to spread Russian culture and language among non-Russian—often other Slavic—people. These programs began in Russia in the late eighteenth century but gained in their importance beginning in the 1860s. The idea of Russification and its goals were also very popular in the former Soviet Union republics from the 1930s until 1991 when the union was dissolved.

4   For more on the Eurasian Steppe, see Warwick Ball, *The Erasian Steppe: People, Movement, Ideas* (Edinburgh University Press, 2022).

5   There are two main sources for Holodmor, a book and a reader: *The Holodomor: The History and Legacy of the Ukrainian Famine Engineered by the Soviet Union* (Charles River Editors, 2020); Bohdan Klid and Alexander J. Motyl, eds., *The Holodomor Reader: A Sourcebook on the Famine of 1932–1933 in Ukraine* (CIUS Press, 2012).

6   The best biography of Stepan Bandera remains Grzegorz Rossolinski, *Stepan Bandera: The Life and Afterlife of a Ukrainian Nationalist: Fascism, Genocide, and Cult* (Moscow: ibidem Press, 2014).

7   Grzegorz Rossolinski-Liebe, "Putin's Abuse of History: Ukrainian 'Nazis,' 'Genocide,' and Fake Threat Scenario," *Journal of Slavic Military Studies* 35, issue 1, 2022.

8   For more on the Soviet and Russian presidents before Vladimir Putin, see Timothy Snyder, *On Tyranny: Twenty Lessons from the Twentieth*

Century (Washington: Crown Books, 2017); and an audible book by
Steven Lee Myers, narrated by Rene Ruiz, *The New Tsar: The Rise
and Reign of Vladimir Putin* (Random House Audio, 2015).

9   When I use the name of the city in Ukraine and the original Slavic
kingdom, I will refer to them as *Kiev* and the *Kievan Rus'*. The major
primary source for the latter term is what has come to be called the
Russkaya Pravda, or the "Russian Primary Source." In my analysis, I
have relied on the Cambridge University version of that text, published
in 2020. Secondary sources for Part One include the following:
Vladimir Volkoff, *Vladimir: The Russian Viking* (Woodstock:
Overlook Press, 1985); Jukka Korpela, *Prince, Saint, and Apostle:
Prince Vladimir of Kiev* (Munich: Wiesbaden Harrasowitz, 2001);
John Breck, *The Legacy of St. Vladimir* (Yonkers: St. Vladimir's
Press, 1990); and Francis Butler, *Enlightener of Rus'* (Bloomington:
University of Indiana Press, 2002). For more on the Russkaya Pravda,
see *Russkaya Pravda. Aforizmy* (Olma Media Group, 2013, Russian
edition), and *Russkaya Pravda*, an English paperback published by
Betascript. Also see *Pravda, Vyplyvshaya Naruszhu* (2003).
The Ruthenians or Ruthene come from the Latin noun, Rutheni that
was used in the late medieval and early modern periods to designate
all eastern Slavs of the Grand Duchy of Lithuania and for people of the
former Kievan Rus, that is, Russians, Ukrainians and Belarusians.
The Carpathian-Ruthenia, or Karpatska Rus' in Russian, is a historical
region on the border between central and eastern Europe, mostly in
western Ukraine, eastern Slovakia, and the Lemko region of Poland.
During the Middle Ages, the region was part of the Kevan Rus'
empire. Hungary, in the tenth century, conquered the Carpathian Basin
and held it until the end of World War I. Between the two world wars,
it was part of Czechoslovakia.

10   *Russkaya Pravda*, 1–19.

11   A monument to Vladimir the Red Sun was erected in Moscow on
November 4, 2016.

12   *Russkaya Pravda*, 18–19.

13   John Breck, *The Legacy of St. Vladimir* (Yonkers: St. Vladimir's Press,
1990), 17–23.

14   Molosh, or Mokosa, among the Slavs was the Mother Goddess and
Goddess of Fertility and the Protector of Women. She also determined
the fate of women and is said to have dabbled in sorcery. Later, among

some Slavs, Molosh was also worshipped as the "Ruler Over Death."

15   Breck, 22–23.

16   For more on early Russian polytheism, see Nancy Shields Kollmann, *The Russian Empire:1450–1801* (Oxford: Oxford University Press, 2017).

17   Ibid., Jukka Korpela, *Prince, Saint, and Apostle: Prince Vladimir of Kiev* (Munich: Wiesbaden Harrassowitz, 2001), 233–235.

18   Ibid., 300. The myth of the Great Storm is sometimes also associated with the Great Flood of the early chapters of Genesis.

19   Korpela, 23–27.

20   The Church of the Tithes was built by Vladimir between 989 and 996, mostly by Byzantine local workers. It was built to commemorate the Baptism of Kievan Rus'. The church of Hagia Sophia in Istanbul was first dedicated in 360 by Emperor Constantius, son of Emperor Constantine. It served as the "cathedra" or Bishop's seat. It was originally known as the "Megale Ekklesia" or "Great Church." It was destroyed around 430 CE and rebuilt by Emperor Justinian and dedicated on December 27, 537.

21   Korpela, 27.

22   Breck, 47. For more on the death of prince Vladimir, see Georges Boisclair, *Saint Volodymyr: The Beautiful Sun, Grand Prince of Kiev, 958–1015* (Winnipeg: Volodymyr Publishing House, 1988); Francis Butler, *Enlightener of Rus': The Image of Vladimir Sviatoslavich across the Centuries* (Indiana: Slavica, 2002); and Vladimir Volkoff, *Vladimir the Russian Viking: The Legendary Prince Who Transformed a Nation* (New York: Overlook Books, 1985).

23   The Monastery of the Caves is a major Orthodox monastery in Kiev. It was founded in the time of the Kievan Rus' around 1050. A monk called the Venerable Anthony is credited as its founder when he first settled in one of the caves. Now known as the "Far Caves" or the "Caves of Theodosius."

24   In this sense, many attributed the life of Vladimir itself to be a miracle.

25   Saint Volodymyr's Cathedral in Kiev is one of the most beautiful churches in all of Europe. The most recent version was built in the nineteenth century to commemorate the nine-hundredth anniversary of Russian baptizing. Russian Emperor Nicholas I approved of the project. The cathedral has seven domes that are fifty meters high. This spelling of the cathedral in Kiev and President Zelensky's name

as well, is an indication that "Volodymyr" is spelled differently in Ukrainian. Prince Vladimir I was known as the Baptizer because he accepted the Orthodox Christian Church as the "religion of his lands" in 988. The event is recorded in the *Primary Chronicle*. Not only did he accept baptism for himself, but he also called on the people of Kiev to be baptized in the Dnieper River. Vladimir's twelve sons were baptized o the same day as himself. Then, the next day, the residents of Kiev were called to the river, where Orthodox priests completed the sacrament of baptism. For more on these events, see John Meyendorff, *Byzantium and the Rise of Russia* (New York: St. Vladimir's Seminary Press, 1989). The copy of the *Russian Chronicle* used for this study is the Thunder Bay Press edition, published in 2001. Also see Wikipedia's "Christianization of Kievan Rus'," https://bit.ly/3cUk32p.

26 Volkoff, 99–113. Photius of Constantinople (820–893) was the ecumenical patriarch of Constantinople from 858 to 867 and again from 877 until 866. He is recognized by the Eastern Orthodox Church as Saint Photius the Great. Next to John Chrysostom in the fifth century, Photius is recognized as the most powerful and influential church leader of Constantinople.

27 The "Passion Bearers" are considered the first martyrs of the Russian Orthodox Church. See Breck, 100–106.

28 Olga of Kiev was born around 890. She married Prince Igor I in 903 CE. For the most part, she raised her grandson, Prince Vladimir. Saint Olga of Kiev (890–969) was the grandmother of Prince Vladimir I of Kievan Rus'. She was married to Igor of Kiev and is known for her subjugation of the Drevlians, a tribe who had killed her husband. Olga is venerated as a saint in the Eastern Orthodox Church with the epithet "Equal to the Apostles." Her feast day is July 11. For more on Saint Olga of Kiev, see Ivan Katchanovski, *Historical Dictionary of Ukraine* (Maryland: Scarecrow Press, 2005); and the *Encyclopedia Britannica*, 1911, vol. 20, 11th ed., p. 80.

29 Prince Vladimir is also sometimes referred to among the Slavs as the "Thirteenth Apostle."

30 For more on the etymology of the word Russia, see Korpela, 63–72; and Butler, ch. 1.

31 Ibid.

32 From the end of the eighth century until the middle of the eleventh century, the Vikings were one of the most prominent forces in all of

Europe. They left a lasting impression as fierce warriors and skilled seamen who we still hear tales of today. Those Eastern Slavs who participated in Viking raids of Byzantium and across the Caspian Sea were technically "Vikings." Neither Byzantium nor the Arabs, however, used that term to refer to Kievan Rus'. Basil II (957–1025) was the Byzantine Emperor from 976 to 1025. He extended the imperial rule in the Balkans, particularly Bulgaria, and he married his sister Anna off to Vladimir I of Kievan Rus'. The marriage was only secured with the promise that Prince Vladimir—like his grandmother Olga—would convert to Christianity.

33   The date of the empire's most extensive extent is generally given as 1051 CE. Yaroslav the Wise (978–1054), whose Christian name was George, was the eldest son of Vladimir and the Prince of Kiev and Novgorod.

34   Andrew Louth, *Greek East and Latin West: The Church AD 681–1071* (New York: St. Vladimir's Seminary Press, 2007), 159.

35   See Vladimir Putin's remarks from November 4, 2016. He also made similar remarks on July 20, 2019, and most recently on February 21, 2022, at the opening of the present hostilities in Ukraine, and on March 17, 2022, one month into the current war. All the way back to a speech of Putin's on August 30, 2014, in an article for *Vox* called, "The Single most important Sentence in Putin's New Comments on Ukraine," Fisher related that the sentence in question was "The Russian and Ukrainian peoples are practically one single people."

36   Korpela, ch. 1, 1–6. Also see Kollmann, 21–128. The term "Dark Ages" is not to be confused with the Western Christian Dark Ages from 500 until about the year 1000.

37   The two works we have relied upon the most in Part Two are Larry Slawson, *The Mongol Invasion of Russia* (Kindle Books, 2019); and Edward D. Sokol, *The Mongol Invasion of Russia* (New York: Allied Books, 1990).

38   Edward D. Sokol, *The Mongol Invasion of Russia* (New York: Allied Books, 1990), 11.

39   Ibid.

40   Sokol, 19–20.

41   Ibid., 20.

42   Ibid., 22. For more on the name Temuchin, see Hayden Chakra, "From Temuchin to Genghis Khan (1167–1227)" *About History*, May 1,

2021, https://bit.ly/3PZk6rO.

43   Ibid., 9.

44   Slawson, 37.

45   For more on the Eurasian steppe, see *National Geographic Encyclopedia* entry for "Steppe," https://bit.ly/3zmQfma

46   Sokol, 46.

47   For more on the Golden Hoard, see Geraldine McCaughrean, *The Golden Hoard: Myths and Legends of the World* (Cambridge: Cambridge University Press, 1996).

48   Ibid, 47–49.

49   Ibid., 49.

50   For more on the establishment of the Duchy of Moscow, see Zh. Marzheret, *The Conditions of the Russian State and the Grand Duchy of Moscow* (London: Books on Demand, 2015).

51   Ibid., 18.

52   Sokel, 63.

53   For more on the Polish-Lithuanian Commonwealth, see Richard Butterwick, *The Polish-Lithuanian Commonwealth* (New Haven: Yale University Press, 2021). The colonies of the republics of Venice and Genoa were a series of economic and political trade posts in the Mediterranean and Black Seas in the fourteenth century. Some were established with local merchants by republican authorities from the two Italian kingdoms, especially during the Crusades, while others originated as feudal possessions of Venetian and Genoese noblemen, or they had been established by powerful, private institutions like the Bank of Saint George.

54   Ibid., 111.

55   Sokel, 70–71.

56   For more on Gediminas, see S. C. Rowell, *Lithuania Ascending* (Cambridge: Cambridge University Press, 1994). Also see the article in the *New World Encyclopedia*, https://bit.ly/3oGONWX.

57   Ibid., 43.

58   Ibid., 45–46.

59   Ibid., 47. Ivan III, also called Ivan Veliky or Ivan the Great (1440–1505), was the Grand Prince of Moscow from 1462 until 1505, at his death. He subdued most of the historical Russian lands simply by the voluntary agreement of princes from the Polish-Lithuanian Federation. He also repudiated the old subservience to the Mongol-derived Tartars.

Ivan Veliky also laid the administrative foundations for the later centralized Russian state.

60   For more on the early czars of Russia, see Daniel B. Rowland, *God, Tsar and People: The Political Culture of Early Modern Russia* (Chicago: Northern Illinois University Press, 2020), particularly chapters one and two.

61   Pyotr Veliky, or Peter the Great (1672–1725), was a czar of Russia who reigned with his half-brother, Ivan V (1682–1696), and then alone afterward from 1696 until 1725. In 1721, Peter was proclaimed Imperator, or Emperor. He was one of Russia's greatest statesmen, organizers and political reformers. For more on Peter the Great, see Mark Steinberg, *A History of Russia: From Peter the Great to Gorbachev* (Cambridge: Harvard University Press, 2000), especially chapter one.

62   For more on the history of the czars in Russia, see Peter Waldron, *Russia of the Tsars* (London: Thames and Hudson, 2011).

63   The two main sources relied on in constructing Part Three of this essay were Robert H. Wilde, *The Russian Revolution* (Independently published, 2018); and Orlando Figes, *A People's Tragedy: The Russian Revolution: 1891–1924* (Pengiun Books, 1998).

64   For more on the causes of the Revolution, see chapters one and two of Figes, *A People's Tragedy: The Russian Revolution: 1891–1924.*

65   Ibid., 26–33.

66   Alexander Samsonov (1858–1914) oversaw the Russian military disaster at the Battle of Tannenberg but originally served as a cavalry officer after graduating from the Russian Military Academy in St. Petersburg. Samsonov also saw service in the Russo-Turkish War of 1877 and 1878. In fact, for a while, he was governor of Turkestan. He died in military action in 1914 in East Prussia at the beginning of Russia's involvement in World War I. For more on Alexander Samsonov, see John J. Jacobson, *All the Cowboys Ain't Gone* (New York: Blackstone Publishing, 2021).

67   For more on Russia and World War I: see Steven Fisher, *Into Russia's Cauldron* (New York: Forest Cat Books, 2021).

68   Ibid., 29–31.

69   Wilde, 27–43.

70   For more on Alexandra's German background, see C. F. Yetmen, *The Roses Underneath* (Kindle Books, 2014).

71 For more on Rasputin, see Aron Simanovitch, *Rasputin: The Memoirs of his Secretary* (Kindle Editions, 2013).

72 Ibid., 100–102.

73 Ibid., quoted on p. 103.

74 Ibid.

75 Wilde, 96.

76 Figes, 61.

77 Ibid.

78 Ibid., 62–63. Leon Trotsky (1879–1940) was a leading Marxist revolutionary in the first half of the twentieth century. He played key roles in the 1905 revolution, as well as the 1917 Bolshevik Revolution. Late in his life, he was exiled to Mexico, where he had an affair with artist Frida Kahlo. In Mexico, he also became a chicken farmer and finally was assassinated by an agent of Josef Stalin in August of 1940 with an ice pick through his eye.

79 For more on the Russian White Guard, see Mikhail Bulgakov, *The White Guard* (Kindle Editions, 2012).

80 Ibid., 39.

81 Ibid.

82 For more on Stalin's "Red Terror," consult Peter Whitewood, *The Red Army and the Great Terror* (Lawrence: University Press of Kansas, 2015).

83 Wilde, 92–95.

84 Ibid., 98.

85 Whitewood, 77.

86 Wilde, 111.

87 We will speak more about this issue in Parts Four and Five of this essay.

88 This timeline was constructed from Wilde and Figes.

89 For more on Hitler's invasion of Russia: see David M. Glantz, *Operation Barbarossa: Hitler's Invasion of Russia* (Kindle Editions, 2011).

90 Ibid., 34–38.

91 Ibid., 38.

92 Ibid.

93 Ibid., 39–40.

94 Ibid., 40.

95 For more on the Battle of Stalingrad, see *Stalingrad: A Captivating*

Guide to the Battle of Stalingrad and Its Impact on World War II (Captivating History, 2020). For a more German perspective of the battle, consult: Jonathan Trigg, *The Battle of Stalingrad Through German Eyes* (Kindle Editions, 2022). The Russian T-34 medium tank was introduced in 1940. Its 76.2 mm tank gun was more powerful than any of its contemporaries. It also had a sixty-degree sloped armor to provide protection from anti-tank weapons. The T-34 also incorporated the design of American J. Walter Christie turret-less tank that he sold to the Red Army after being rejected by the US Army.

96   Ibid., 63–67.

97   Josef Stalin was named *Time* magazine's "Man of the Year" in 1939 and again in 1942. The award has since been renamed "Person of the Year." Interestingly enough, Nikita Khrushchev in 1957 and Vladimir Putin in 2007 were also chosen for the award.

98   Kaleena Fraga, "How Many People Did Stalin Kill?" *All That's Interesting*, May 13, 2022, https://bit.ly/3BGHYf6.

99   The Soviet Republics were the following: Armenia, Azerbaijan, Belarus, Estonia, Georgia, Kazakhstan, Kyrgyz, Latvia, Lithuania, Moldova, Russia, Tajik, Turkmenistan, Ukraine and Uzbekistan.

100   Boris Yeltsin (1931–2007) served as president from 1991 to 1999. Though a Communist party member for most of his life, in the end, he believed in both democracy and the free market system.

101   Mr. Putin's time as the interim president was from 1999 to 2000. His first term as president was from 2000 to 2004. His second term was from 2004 to 2008. He was prime minister from 2008 to 2012 and president for this third term from 2012 to 2018. He proposed a constitutional amendment in 2020, so he could serve a fourth term from 2020 to 2024.

102   This is related to a three-prong approach that Mr. Putin learned from Josef Stalin, which we will extensively discuss in Part Five of this essay.

103   Mr. Zelenskyy was elected on April 21, 2019. His tenure will run until 2023 and then run again for only one more term.

104   Mr. Trump was impeached by the House of Representatives on February 5, 2020.

105   This summary of the Cold War was gleaned from two sources: Odd Arne Westad, *The Cold War* (New York: Basic Books, 2019); and John Lewis Gaddis, *The Cold War: A New History* (New York: Penguin

Books, 2006).

106 For more on the Truman Doctrine, see Denise M. Bostdorff, *Proclaiming the Truman Doctrine* (Dallas: Texas A&M University Press, 2008); Richard M. Freeland, *The Truman Doctrine and the Origins of McCarthyism: Foreign Policy, Domestic Politics, and Internal Security, 1946–1948* (New York: Knopf, 1972); and an anonymous text called *Legislative Origins of the Truman Doctrine* (Forgotten Books, 2018).

107 This containment period had more significant events than any of the other five periods.

108 Gaddis, 77.

109 The Warsaw Pact was officially signed on May 14, 1955. It included eight original members: the Soviet Union, Albania, Poland, Romania, Hungary, East Germany, Czechoslovakia, and Bulgaria. The Alliance remained intact until 1991.

110 For more on the Cuban missile crisis, consult: Norman Polmer, *Defcon-2: Standing on the Brink of Nuclear War During the Cuban Missile Crisis* (Oxford: Wiley, 2006); and Robert F. Kennedy, *Thirteen Days: A Memoir of the Cuban Missile Crisis* (New York: Norton, 1999). Premier Nikita Khrushchev was ousted from office and as head of the Soviet Communist Party on October 14, 1964, after ten years of being in power. He was succeeded by his former protégé, Leonid Brezhnev. One of the reasons for Khrushchev's downfall was the cost of the military support of the North Vietnamese Army; while Ronald Reagan and the United States were in the process of an arms buildup in the 1980s, Khrushchev and Brezhnev, as well as later Soviet leaders, like Mikhail Gorbachev, ran out of money.

111 The French withdrew from NATO's military structures on March 11, 1959.

112 The period of Détente was officially from 1969 until 1979. It began with the signing of the nuclear nonproliferation treaty in late 1968 and continued until Russia's withdraw from Afghanistan in 1979.

113 The new Cold War period was during the two terms of President Ronald Reagan, from 1980 until 1988.

114 Albania withdrew from the Warsaw Pact in 1968, but it had not actively participated since 1961.

115 The dissolving of the Warsaw Pact officially occurred on December 31, 1991, a week after the dissolution of the Soviet Union.

116   The Collective Security Treaty members were Russia, Belarus, Armenia, Kazakhstan, Kyrgyzstan, Tajikistan and Uzbekistan. In 2002, it changed its name to the Collective Security Treaty Organization (CSTO).

117   In this period, all but Kazakhstan had withdrawn from the CSTO.

118   This list of factors was developed by my son, John "Jack" Vicchio, an astute student of both world history in general and Russian history in particular.

119   On August 1, 1991, all fifteen former Soviet states besides Russia had withdrawn.

120   We have gleaned these causes for the collapse of the Soviet Union from several essays in *The Collapse of the Soviet Union*, which also has an audiobook version narrated by Colin Fluxman.

121   Felix Dzerzhinsky (1877–1926) was the founder of the Bolshevik secret police, a forerunner to the KGB.

122   For more on perestroika, see Bill Keller, "New Struggle in the Kremlin: How to Change the Economy," *New York Times*, June 4, 1987; and Mr. Gorbachev's own book *Perestroika: New Thinking for Our Country and the World* (New York: Harper Collins, 1987).

123   For more on Stalin's five-year plans, consult: Nick Shepley, *Stalin, the Five-Year Plans and the Gulags* (London: AUK Academic, 2013).

124   This movement in Poland was called the "Solidarity Movement." For more on the Polish Solidarity Movement, see Maryjane Osa, *Solidarity and Contention: Networks of Polish Opposition* (Minneapolis: University of Minnesota Press, 2003); and Robert Brier, *Poland's Solidarity Movement and the Global Politics of Human Rights* (Cambridge: Cambridge University Press, 2021).

125   These six republics were Armenia, Estonia, Georgia, Latvia, Moldova and Lithuania.

126   This, of course, was a trumped-up way for Boris Yeltsin and his cronies to begin their plan to take over.

127   Mr. Gobachev delivered this speech on August 22, 1991, three days after the tank address. But again, it is not clear that the words were actually his. The Soviet flag that flew over the Kremlin was lowered for the final time on December 25, 1991, at 7:32 p.m. The pre-Revolutionary flag of white, blue and red horizontal stripes took its place. It was only witnessed by a handful of foreign visitors and one irate Soviet Army veteran on Red Square, according to the *New York*

Times on December 26, 1991.

128 By the "Perestroika period," we mean the reign of Mikhail Gorbachev from roughly 1986 until May 1988.

129 For the life of Vladimir Putin, we have relied on two principal sources: Steven Lee Myers, narrated by René Ruiz, *The New Tsar: The Rise and Reign of Vladimir Putin* (Random House Audio, 2015); and Vladimir Putin's autobiographical work entitled *First Person: An Astonishingly Frank Self-Portrait by Russia's President* (Washington: Public Affairs Editions, 2000).

130 Myers, 17–20.

131 Ibid., 20.

132 Putin, 19–23.

133 Myers, 50.

134 Ibid., 52.

135 For more on the Malaysia Airlines flight, see "Russia Keen to Thwart Investigation," *The Guardian*, March 10, 2020.

136 Russia's incursion in Crimea continued with no change.

137 Report from the United Nations on the Russian incursion of Crimea, September 22, 2015, https://bit.ly/3SmzQqH.

138 Mr. Putin's address before the United Nations was on September 28, 2015. For more on this speech, see "In Assembly address, Russia president stresses national sovereignty within the context of UN Charter," *UN News*, September 28, 2015, https://bit.ly/3Qfy60u.

139 Mr. Putin abandoned his plans to capture Kiev on April 20, 2022.

140 Vladimir Putin's speech to demilitarize and de-Nazify Ukraine was on February 18, 2022, six days before the war began.

141 For more on Stepan Bandera, consult Grzegorz Rossolinski-Liebe, *Stepan Bandera: The Life and Afterlife of a Ukrainian Nationalist* (Kindle Editions, 2014).

142 Ibid., chapters 2 and 3.

143 Vladimir Putin speech, March 18, 2022.

144 The Sergey Lavrov and Sergei Naryshkin quotations were taken from Paul Kirby, "Ukraine conflict: Who's in Putin's inner circle and running the war?" *BBC News*, March 3, 2022, https://bbc.in/3vFknIp.

145 Mr. Zelenskyy made these comments on not being a Nazi on March 18, 2022.

146 Ibid.

147 The expression "the liberation of Donbas" was used by Putin and other

Russian officials on March 24, 2022.

148 We have borrowed these three reasons from chapter 5 of Myers.

149 The 1654 treaty, the Pereiaslav Agreement, was formalized while a Cossack delegation was visiting Moscow in March. It established the tzar's protectorate over the Cossacks. The name comes from the name of the town where it was signed.

150 See Note 115.

151 Ukraine last conducted joint military actions with NATO in early April 2021.

152 This provision of the NATO charter can be found in Article Five of that charter.

153 Mr. Putin made this remark on December 11, 2021.

154 Ibid.

155 We speak here of Mr. Biden's approval ratings that have hovered around 30 percent for six months, beginning in January of 2022. Eight months later, since January of 2022, President Biden's approval rating has begun to rise to 42.7 percent on September 2, 2022. His disapproval rating, however, is still at 52.8 percent.

156 These activities began in presidential orders starting on January 20, 2021. For more on President Biden's canceling of the Keystone Pipeline contract, see David Blackmon, *Why Biden's Killing of Keystone XL was an Energy Security Blunder*, https://bit.ly/3xaxuCl, March 10, 2022. Mr. Blackmon is a Texas-based public policy analyst.

157 For more on the Trans-Dniester Region, see "Trans-Dniester Region," *The Columbia Electronic Encyclopedia* (Columbia University Press, 2012), https://bit.ly/3A08U8X.

158 This issue on the relation of Russian oil and gasoline, its exportation and its prices, could be the subject of another study in its own right.

159 Lenin, V. I., "About the Attitudes of the Working Party Toward Religion," *Collected Works*, vol. 17, 41.

160 Marx, Karl, *Critique of Hegel's 'Philosophy of Right'* (Cambridge: Cambridge University Press, 1977).

161 Russian Federation Constitution. July 10, 1918.

162 Ibid.

163 Anderson, John, Religion, State and Politics in the Soviet Union and Successor States. (Cambridge: Cambridge University Press, 1994), 2.

164 CNA Staff, "Things to know About the Catholic Church in Ukraine," National Catholic Register, February 24, 2022, https://bit.ly/3Vk1ndQ.

165 Quay, Grayson, "War in Ukraine is a 'metaphysical' battle against a civilization built on 'gay parades,' Russian Orthodox leader says," The Week, March 7, 2022, https://bit.ly/3CRiT1T.

166 Paul Elie, "The Long Holy War Behind Putin's Political War in Ukraine," The New Yorker, April 21, 2022, https://bit.ly/3Tfxfyp.

167 Ibid.

168 O'Beara, Fearghas, "Russia's war on Ukraine: The religious dimension," European Parliament, April 2022, https://bit.ly/3SOoUSt.

169 Ibid.

170 Ibid.

171 Arnold, Victoria, "Russian Religious Communities Opposed to Ukraine War Face Pressure and Censorship," Religion Unplugged, May 16, 2022, https://bit.ly/3ECa9Ou.

172 Ibid.

173 Ibid.

174 Psalm 34:14, Author's translation.

175 Arnold.

176 Will Vernon, "Ukraine war: Russia appeals for new recruits for war effort." BBC News, August 22, 2022, https://bbc.in/3TvlSDy.

177 Ibid.

178 Ibid.

179 M. Shabandeh, "Carnegie Supernova Project." Astrophysical (2021).

180 Ibid.

181 Ibid.

182 Ibid.

183 Ibid.

184 Ibid.

185 Ibid.

186 Ibid.

187 "Ukrainian War in Maps: Tracking the Russian Invasion," BBC, https://bbc.in/3LhexUg. "Interactive Map: Russia's Invasion of Ukraine," Institute for the Study of War, https://bit.ly/3U9Q5rY.

188 The Revoliutsiia hidnosti, of "Revolution of Dignity," took place at the end of the Euromaidan protests when clashes between Russian separatists and the Ukrainian Army occurred. This culminated in the ousting of Pro-Russian President Viktor Yanukovych.

189 For more on the removal of Viktor Yanukovych from the presidency, see Michael Ray, "Viktor Yanukovych," Britannica, July 5, 2022, https://bit.ly/3e792Lm.

190 For more on the Minsk II agreement, see Duncan Allan, *The Minsk Conundrum: Western Policy and Russia's War in Eastern Ukraine* (London: Chatham House, 2020), https://bit.ly/3wKq4oW.

191 The "Six-Day War" is also called the "June War" or the "Arab-Israeli War" or *Naksah*. It took place from June 5 to 10, 1967. In the war, Israel successfully captured the Sinai Peninsula, the Gaza Strip, the West Bank, the Old City of Jerusalem, and the Golan Heights. For more on the Six Day War, see Juan Marcos Bejarano Gutierrez, *The Six Day War: A Concise Introduction to the War that Changed the Middle East* (Jerusalem: Yaron Publishing, 2018). I have also consulted an unbridged audiobook written by Michael B. Oren and narrated by Robert Whitfield entitled *Six Days of War: June 1967 and the Making of the Modern Middle East*, produced by Blackstone Audio in 2005.

192 Carl Von Clausewitz (1780–1831) was a Prussian general and military theorist. His most famous work, and the place where we find this idea of the importance of public assent to a war, is his *Vom Kriege*, or "On War," which was unfinished at his death.

193 Peter A. Wilson and William Courtney, "What if Russia's army fails in Ukraine?" *The Hill*, June 19, 2022, https://bit.ly/3Q4ewnl.

194 Anonymous, "UN alarm as Ukraine nuclear power plant shelled again," *BBC News*, August 12, 2022, https://bbc.in/3AWKz4l.

195 Ibid.

196 Ibid.

197 Ibid.

198 Ibid.

199 Mr. Zelensky quoted in Leonie Chao-Fong, et al. "Russia-Ukraine war latest: what we know on day 185 of the invasion," *The Guardian*, August 26, 2022, https://bit.ly/3wLuUT8.

200 Ibid. The article quoted the *Wall Street Journal* report from the same day.

201 Anonymous, "GDP Forecasts, 2022, % Change on a Year Earlier," *The Economist*, August 29, 2022.

202 This is the language reported in an article in the *Sky News* on August 28, 2022. The article quotes Dmitry Peskov, Mr. Putin's press secretary.

203 According to figures from July 27, 2022, Poland had taken in 5 million refugees; Russia, 1,800,000; Hungary, a million; Romania, 890,000;

Slovakia, 625,000; Moldova, 580,000; and Belarus, 17,000.

204   Lugansk, with a population of over 300,000, has traditionally been
       a city of iron mills. It was originally founded on the Lugan River
       in 1795. Donetsk was founded by a Welsh businessman in 1869,
       principally to exploit the coal mines in the southern region of the
       Russian Empire.

205   In September 2015, President Putin ordered the Russian military to
       intervene on behalf of Syrian President Bashar Al-Assad, who was in
       the fifth year of the civil war in Syria. For more on Russia in Syria in
       2015, see Tom Cooper, *Moscow's Game of Poker: Russian Military
       Intervention in Syria, 2015–2017* (Helion and Company, 2022).

206   The Soviets were involved in a war in Afghanistan from 1979 until
       1989. It was mostly a conflict between the Mujahideen and smaller
       Marxist groups against the Democratic Republic of Afghanistan.
       Svetlana Alexievich, *Zinky Boys: Soviet Voices from the Afghanistan
       War* (New York: W. W. Norton, 1992); and Lester Grau, ed., *The
       Bear Went Over the Mountain: Soviet Combat Tactics in Afghanistan*
       (Fourth Watch Publishing, 2021), narrated by Luis Ayala. This audio
       book is nearly six hours long and covers much about Russia's ten-year
       involvement in Afghanistan.

207   Mr. Putin told an aide on February 29, 2022, that the war would be
       over by March 15.

208   On May 31, 2022, Ukraine officials claimed that at least 30,500
       Russian soldiers had been killed in the war.

209   The Kherson province of Ukraine, with a population of 1,125,000,
       contain eight cities and twenty-nine urban-type residential areas.

210   The story of David and Goliath can be found in First Samuel, chapter
       seventeen.

211   We garnered these three solutions from an article in the *New Yorker* by
       Isaac Chotiner on March 9, 2022, https://bit.ly/3QawF3I.

212   Ibid.

213   Ibid.

214   Ibid.

215   Ibid.

216   Ibid.

217   At the 2008 Bucharest Summit, Ukraine and Georgia were promised
       eventual membership in NATO.

218   Mr. Biden called for a "regime change" in Russia on March 27, 2022.

Later, his White House walked back the comment and said that was not what he was doing.

219   Nine countries in the world have nuclear weapons. Russia has the most (6,270), followed by the US (5,550), China (359), France (290), the UK (225), Pakistan (165), India (156), Israel (90), and North Korea (40 to 50).

220   Moldovan leaders, such as Prime Minister Natalia Gavrilita, in several interviews with the Western press, is convinced that her country is next in line after Ukraine.

221   Anton Troianovski, "Russia's Retreat in Ukraine Pokes Holes in Putin's Projection of Force," *New York Times*, September 11, 2022.

222   Ibid.

223   Ibid.

224   Ibid.

225   Ibid.

226   Ibid.

227   Kostan Nechyporenko, "Ukrainian official: More Than Forty Settlements in the Kharkiv Region Liberated," *CNN News*, September 11, 2022.

228   Ibid.

229   President Zelensky's daily news conference in Kiev, September 11, 2022.

230   Kostan Nechyporenko, "Ukrainian official: More Than Forty Settlements in the Kharkiv Region Liberated," *CNN News*, September 11, 2022.

231   The term "crimes against humanity," an offense in international criminal law, was adopted in the Charter of the International Military Tribunal in Nuremberg, Germany, in 1945. Several Nazi leaders were charged with crimes against humanity, as well as some leaders in 1998 in the International Criminal Court. For more on the Nuremberg Tribunal and Nuremberg Trials, see *The Nuremberg Trials: Complete Tribunal Proceedings* (e-artnow, 2022); and Francine Hirsch, *Soviet Judgment at Nuremberg: A New History of the International Military Tribunal After World War II* (New York: Oxford University Press, 2022).

232   In an interview on April 4, 2022, Mr. Biden expressed his opinion that Russia committed war crimes in Ukraine. At the time, he said to *Al-Jezeera*, "You may remember I was criticized for calling Putin a war

criminal. Well, the truth of the matter is, we saw it happen in Bucha… he is a war criminal."

233 Ambassador Beth Van Schaack, speech on the Ukraine war, June 10, 2022, https://bit.ly/3QElwbA.

Index

Page numbers in italics
refer to images

A

Adriatic Sea 18
Afghanistan 57–59, 116
Albania 58
Alexander, Grand Duke
    of Lithuania 22
Alexander I 28
Alexander II 28
Alexander III 28, 44
Alexandra, Czarina 34,
    36, *38*, 39, 44, 50,
    96
Alexis I 28
Algirdas, General 22
Allies 33, 48, 51, 96, 119
Ancient Russians 5
Andropov, Yuri 3, 59
Angola 59
Anna, Czarina 28, 95
annexation 1, 14, 17, 24,
    30, 55, 73, 108
Arabs 12–14, 94
Armenia 43
Aryans 46
Asia 18, 94, 100
Assad, Bashar al- 71,
    116
atheism 84–85, 87
Azerbaijan 43

B

Balkans 7, 18

Bandera, Stepan 2, 72
Bartholomew I 89
Bashkirs 100–101
Basil II 8–9, 13, 93
Battle of Berestovov 10
Battle of Stalingrad 48
Battle of Tannenberg 35
Beijing, China 18
Belarus 5, 20, 54, 71, 88,
    121
Belgium 46
Berlin Blockade and
    Airlift 57
Biden Administration 3,
    119, 125
Biden, Joe 3, 55, 69,
    75–76, 79, 116,
    119–120, 124–125
Black Sea 11, 54, 117–119
Blitzkrieg 46
Bloody Sunday 41, 44,
    50, 96, 127
Bohun Brigade 122
Bolsheviks 34, 40, 43, 45,
    50, 95–96
Boris, son of Vladimir I
    12
Borodin, Pavel 70
breadbasket of the world
    36
Brezhnev, Leonid 57, 59
Bucha, Ukraine 69, 76
Budapest, Hungary 58
Bulgaria 19, 79
Byzantine Empire 8, 22,
    25

C

Capitalist 41
Carpatho-Ruthenians 5
Caspian Sea 18, 47
Cathedral of Holy
    Wisdom 9
Catherine I 28, 30, 95
Catherine II, the Great 2,
    24, 28, *29*, 30, 95
Catholic Church 85–86,
    89, 91, 101
    Carpatho-Rusyn Cath-
        olic Church 85
    Ruthenian Catholic
        Church 85–86
    Ukrainian Catholic
        Church 86
Catholics 86, 88–89, 102
Chechen 70
Cheringov 12
Chernenko, Konstantin
    3, 59
China 18, 20, 57, 111, 120
Chisinau, Moldova 78
Church of the Savior 10
Church of the Tithes *8*, 9
Clausewitz, Carl von 110
Cold War 3, 51, 53,
    56–58, 64–65,
    74–75, 97
Collective Security Treaty
    Organization 58
Commission of Catholic
    Bishops 89
Communism 61, 72, 88
Communist 33, 41–43,

45, 50, 53–54,
56–57, 59–62,
64, 96, 100
Constantinople 9, 13, 22,
25, 93
Containment 56, 65, 97
Crimea 12, 20, 23, 54–55,
64, 66, 71–73, 75,
77–80, 98, 100–
101, 108, 115–117,
120, 124
Crimean Khanate 20
Crimean Peninsula 21,
54, 86, 109
Crisis and Escalation
56–57, 65, 97
Cuba 33
Cuban Missile Crisis 57
Czechoslovakia 58–59,
63
Czech Republic 58, 105

D

Dark Ages 13–14
De Facto Partition View
118
Demacopoulos, George
89
de-Nazification 2–3, 72
Denmark 94
Derhachi, Ukraine 123
Détente 56–57, 65, 97
Dnieper River 1, 9, 19
Dnieper Valley 12
Dolgoruky, Yuri 10
Donbas region, Ukraine
73, 77, 90, 99,
107–109, 116–118,
124
Donetsk region, Ukraine
73, 108, 116
Dresden, Germany 70
Dvina Bay 47
Dzerzhinsky, Felix 61

E

Eastern Bloc 57–58
Eastern Europe 2, 13, 18,
58–59, 63, 110, 124
Eastern Front 45, 48
Eastern Orthodox
Church 13, 93–94
East Germany 58, 70
East Prussia 35
Egypt 110
Einsatzgruppen 47
Einstein, Albert 33
Elena, ruler of Russia,
mother of Ivan
IV 23
Elizabeth I, Czarina 28,
95
El Salvador 59
Energoatom 110
Engels, Frederick 41
Communist Manifesto
41
English 12, 14
Estonia 53, 60, 74
Esugal, father of Genghis
Khan 18, 126
Eurasian Steppe 2, 18,
20–21
European Union 77–78,
78, 105

F

Feodor III 28
Finland 78, 94
Fordham University 89
Orthodox Christian
Studies Center 89
France 46, 105, 111, 119
Francis, Pope 88
Frederick II 47
French 12, 14, 57, 109,
126, 128
Fyodor 29

G

G7 nations 111
gay parades 90, 102
Gediminas of Lithuania
21, 21
Genghis Khan 17
Genoa, Italy 20
genocide 2–3
Georgetown University
89
Georgia 43, 120
Germans 12, 14, 35,
47–48
Germany 45–48, 58, 70,
105, 111, 119
glasnost 59, 61, 66, 86,
97, 126
Gleb, son of Vladimir
I 12
Godunov, Boris 29
Golden Horde 19–20
Goldston, James A. 115
Gorbachev, Mikhail 3,
53, 58–61, 64–66,
86, 98
Grand Duchy of Lithua-
nia 20–21, 23
Grand Duchy of Moscow
20–21, 24
Great Britain 36, 46
Great Standoff 20
Greece 6, 56
Greeks 14, 94
Gregorian calendar 45,
50, 96
Gudziak, Borys 89
Gullickson, Archbishop
86
guns and butter 61, 62,
66, 97

H

Halych 12

Hama, Syria 71
Hegel, Georg 84
  Philosophy of Right
    83–84
Hitchens, Christopher 33
Hitler, Adolf 2, 45–48,
    46, 51, 96
  Directive 21 / Opera-
    tion Barbarossa
    47–48, 51, 96
  Operation Typhoon 48
holodomor 2, 126
Homs, Syria 71
Hungary 18, 58, 94

I

Industrial Revolution 34,
    50, 96
Interim Period 1–2,
    13–14, 17, 20, 24,
    30, 94
International Atomic
    Energy Agency
    110–111
Iron Curtain 57
Islam 18
Ivan III 20, 22
Ivan IV, the Terrible
    23–25, *26*
Ivan V 28
Ivan VI 28
Izium, Ukraine 122–123

J

Japan 34, 105
Jewish Khazars 9
Jihadist 71
Julian calendar 45, 50, 96
Just War Theory 89, 91

K

Kazakhstan 60, 100
Kazan 23

Kerensky, Alexander 33
Keystone Pipeline 76
KGB 61, 64, 66, 68, 70,
    98, 105, 127
Khan, Akhmat 20
Khan, Batu 2, 18–19, 94,
    126
Khan, Genghis 2, *16*,
    17–19, 94, 126, 128
Khan, Hulega 94, 126
Khan, Jochi 2, 18, 127
Khan, Kublai 20, 127
Khan, Mongke 94, 127
Khan, Ogedei *19*, 94
Kharkiv, Ukraine
    122–123, 151
Kherson, Ukraine 112,
    117, 120
Khorev, Mikhail 83
Khrushchev, Nikita 3,
    57, 62
Khwarazm 18
Kievan Rus' 1, 3, 5–9, *11*,
    11–13, 17–19, 24,
    30, 74, 93–94, 101,
    107
Kirill, Patriarch 87–91,
    102
Kolbin, Gennady 60
Korea 18
Korean War 57
Kozacha Lopan, Ukraine
    123
Kremlin 12, 22, 60,
    65–66, 70, 89, 98,
    127–128

L

Latvia 60, 74
Lavrov, Sergei 2, 72
Left Bank of Ukraine 1
Leningrad Church 87
Leningrad, Russia 47–48,
    70

Lenin, Vladimir 22, *32*,
    34, 40–45, *49*, 50,
    62, 84, 96, 101
Lithuania 21, 53–54, 60,
    74
Lithuanians 1, 14, 17, 20
Luftwaffe 47, 127
Luhansk region, Ukraine
    73, 122
Luxembourg 46
Lviv, Ukraine 44

M

Malaysia Airlines 71
Malenkov, Georgy 3
Mariupol, Ukraine 76
Marshall Plan 57
Marxism 62, 84
Marxist-Leninist 87–88,
    101
Marx, Karl 41, *41*, 43,
    83–84, 87, 101
  Communist Manifesto
    41
Medvedev, Dmitry 54
Mensheviks 40
Middle East 94, 116
Minnekaev, Rustam 78,
    80, 99
Minsk, Belarus 71, 108
Minsk II agreement 108
Moldova 12, 30, 78–80,
    88, 94–95, 99, 101,
    121
Monastery of the Caves
    10
Mongol Horde 24
Mongolian Empire 2, 18
Mongol invasion 17
Mongols 1–2, 12, 14,
    17–21, 24, 30, 94,
    128
monotheistic 17
Moscow Diocese 90

Moscow, Russia 10, 20–25, 45, 47–48, 50–51, 60–61, 64, 66, 70, 78, 96, 98, 127
Mozambique 59
Mozhaysk 21
Muscovite-Lithuanian War 22–23
Muslim Bulgars 9
Myth of the Great Storm 7

N

Namibia 59
Naryshkin, Sergei 72
Nasser, Gamal Abdul 109–110
Six-Day War 109
NATO 56–58, 71–72, 74–76, 78–80, 99, 106–107, 120
Nazarbayev, Nursultan 60
Nazis 2–3, 46–48, 51, 72–73, 96
Nehammer, Karl 76
Neo-Nazi 2
Netherlands 46, 105
Neutrality with Sweeteners Approach 118, 120
New Cold War 56–57, 65, 97
New Economic Policy 43
New Russian Empire Solution 118, 121
Nicaragua 59
Nicholas I 28
Nicholas II 28, 30, 36, *37*, 39, 41, 44–45, 50, 95–96
Nixon, Richard 57
Noble Peace Prize 48, 51

Nordic 10, 14, 93–94
Nordic-Slavic polytheism 10, 13, 93
Norway 94, 105
Nostradamus 17
Novgorod 9–12, 22
nuclear power 110–112
Rosatom 110
Nuremberg 115, 125

O

Oka River 22
Olga, grandmother of Vladimir I 6, 10, 12
Order of Saint Vladimir 10
Organisation for Economic Co-operation and Development 119
Orthodox Christianity 6, 8–10, 74, 85
Eastern Orthodox Church 13, 93–94

P

Paul I 28
perestroika 59, 61, 66, 70, 87, 97, 127
Pereyaslavl, Ukraine 12
Persia 18, 94
Peter II 28
Peter III 28, *29*
Peter the Great 25, *27*, 28, 128
Petrograd 45, 50, 96
Photius 11, 13
Platonov, Father Nikolay 90
Poland 1, 18, 20–21, 24, 43–46, 57–59, 63, 79, 94, 105, 116
Poles 1, 14, 17, 20, 72

Polish-Lithuanian Commonwealth/Federation 1, 24, 28, 30, 43, 95
Polish solidarity movement 57, 59
Politburo 43, 61–62, 66, 97
Polotsk 12
polytheism 6, 9–10, 13, 93
Nordic-Slavic polytheism 10, 13, 93
Slavic polytheism 6, 10, 13, 93
Port of Archangel 47
Port of Astrakhan 47
Putin, Vladimir 2–3, 12–13, 30, *52*, 54–56, 66, *68*, 69–81, 83, 86–91, *92*, 94–95, 98–101, 105–112, *114*, 116–123, 125–126

R

Rasputin, Grigori 34, 39, *40*, 45, 50, 96
Rasputista 48
Reagan, Ronald 53, 57
Red Army 48, 72
Red Terror 43
Revolution of Dignity 107, 127
Right Bank of Ukraine 1–2, 24
River Trosna 22
Romania 58
Romanov czars and czarinas 28
Romanov dynasty 25, 28, 30, 95
Romanov, Michael 25, 95
Romans 14, 94

Rossolinski-Liebe, Grzegorz 2–3
Rurik dynasty 28
Rus'-Byzantine War of 860 AD 11
Russaya Mir 89, 128
Russian Army 36, 39, 44, 50, 90, 96, 107, 109–111, 122–123
Russian Empire 2–3, 24, 28, 30, 43, 73, 79–80, 118, 121–122, 124
Russian Federation Constitution 85–86, 89–90
Russian Orthodox Christianity 2, 10
Russian Orthodox Church 7, 12, 85–88, 91, 101–102
Russian Revolution 2, 22, 24, 28, 30, 33–34, 34, 39–40, 42, 44, 50, 95–96
Russian Social Democratic Labor 40
  Second Party Congress 40
Russification 1–2, 124
Russkaya Pravda 6, 128
Russkiy Mir 88, 128
Russo-Ukrainian War 107–108
Ruthenians 5
Ryazan 12, 22

S

Saint Vladimir's Orthodox Theological Seminary 10
Saint Volodymyr's Cathedral 10
SALT treaties 57

Samsonov, General Alexander 35, 35
Saudi Arabia 111
Scholz, Olaf 79
Severnaya Dvina River 47
Shahbandeh, M. 106–107
Shoigu, Sergei 112, 114
Siberia 18, 48
Sigismund I 23, 23
Slavic Gods
  Dazhbog 6, 126
  Dzbog 6, 126
  Lada 8
  Mokosh 7, 127
  Perun 6–7, 127
  Rod 8, 128
  Semargl 6, 128
  Veles 7, 128
  Yarilo 7
Slavic Orthodox Church 9
Slavs 7–8, 10–11, 14
Slovakia 58
Smolensk 12, 23
Sobchak, Anatoly 70
Socialist 33, 39, 59, 121
Song Dynasty 20
Southeast Asian Treaty Organization 57
South Vietnamese Army 109
Soviet Army 47
Soviet Jews 47
Soviet Union 1–3, 34, 43–47, 51, 53, 57–63, 65–66, 74–75, 79–81, 83, 96–98, 100, 121
Space Race 57
Stalinist 59, 61, 108
Stalin, Josef 2–3, 22, 34, 43, 45, 47–51, 49, 49, 61–63, 66, 79, 81, 85–86, 88,

96–98, 100–101, 120–121, 124
St. Petersburg 27, 41, 44, 70, 79, 98, 127
Sultans of the Ottoman Empire 20–21
Suzdal 12
Svatove, Ukraine 122
Sviatopolk, son of Vladimir I 12
Svyatoslav, Grand Prince of Kiev 6
Sweden 78, 94, 105
Swedish 12, 14
Synod of Lviv 86
Syria 71
Syrian civil war 71, 116

T

Taman peninsula 11
Tartar Hordes 23
Tartars 20, 100–101
Thatcher, Margaret 57
Third Rome 22, 25
Time magazine 48, 51, 97
  Man of the Year 48, 51, 97
Time of Trouble 25, 28–29, 128
Tokarivka, Ukraine 123
Trans-Dniester 78, 80, 99
Treaty of Brest 45
Trotsky, Leon 42, 42
Truman, Harry 56
  Truman Doctrine 56, 65, 97
Trump, Donald 55, 76
Turkey 18, 56, 75
Turks 17
Tver, Russia 22

U

Ugra River 20
Ukraine subdivisions 86

lvano-Frankkivsk 86
Lviv 86
Ternopil 86
Transcarpathia 86
Ukrainian Army 122,
    148
Ukrainian Orthodox
    Church 86, 101,
    130
Ukrainian People's Re-
    public 44
United Nations 71, 76
University of Kiev 10

V

Van Schaack, Beth 115,
    125
Vasily, Emperor of Russia
    23
Venezuela 33
Venice, Italy 20
Vernon, Will 105–106
    BBC News 105
Victoria, Queen 36
Vietnam War 57
Vistula 11
Vladimir I, the Great
    viii, 1, 3, 5–6, 8,
    10–13, 22, 24, 30,
    74, *82*, 87, 93–95,
    101
Vlad the Impaler 105
Volga River 19, 22, 47
Volhyniya 12
Volosovo, Russia 105
Vyazma, Russia 22

W

War in Ukraine 69, 72,
    76, 116, 118
Warsaw Pact 57–58, 74
    Treaty of Friendship,
        Cooperation, and
        Mutual Assistance

57
Washington, DC 75
Western Europe 18,
    46–47
Western Roman Empire
    18
White Guard 43
White Sea 11
Wilson, Peter A. 110
Winter Palace 45, 50, 96
World Council of
    Churches 89, 91
World War I 34, 36, 39,
    44–45, 50, 95
World War II 2–3, 28,
    30, 33, 45, 47–51,
    53, 56, 65, 72–73,
    95–96, 109, 120

Y

Yanukovych, Viktor 108
Yaropolk I 8
Yaroslav I, the Wise *4, 5,*
    10–12, 94
Yeltsin, Boris *52,* 54,
    64–66, 70, 98
Yemen 59, 124
Yugoslavia 63

Z

Zaluzhnyi, General
    Valery 122
Zaporizhzhia, Ukraine
    110–112, 117
Zelensky, Volodymyr
    2–3, 55, *55,* 73,
    76, 93, 111, 116,
    118–120, 123

About the Author

Stephen Vicchio was educated at the University of Maryland, Yale, Oxford, and Saint Andrews University in Fife, Scotland, where he received his Ph.D. He is the author of forty books that include works in drama, stories, essays, religion, philosophy, and books about the Bible. He retired from full-time teaching after having taught in several universities in the United States, Britain, Syria, Egypt, and Portugal, among other places.

Made in the USA
Middletown, DE
29 April 2023

29715723R00102